This journal belongs to

_____

Black Youth are Black Geniuses!

There are centuries of resilience, creativity, wisdom, talent, and intelligence in your DNA – it oozes out of your pores whenever you speak, write, think, or move. Your village must provide the spaces for you to express your rich Black thoughts so that your genius can continue to flourish.

~Dr. Satira 1/13/2021

Black Genius!
• This guided journal was created for you and the village that supports you. It is a place where you can continue to explore the history of your ancestors and elders, while reflecting on who you are today and who you will become in the future.
• Journaling is an opportunity to develop healthy emotional behaviors, feelings, and self-perceptions. The younger you start, the better you will become at reflection and expression.
• Every page has a quote, affirmation, and a writing prompt but the lines are up to you. This is your space! You can respond to what is written or you can express what is on your mind and in your heart for that day.
• The "Black Facts" on each page are designed to pique your curiosity and encourage you to go "deeper" into your past and learn the lessons that rest there.
• This is your personal journal, so make it your own, using your genius to make sense of the world, your history, and yourself.

Special thanks to copy editors Neisha-Ann Greene and Glenda Cohen, interior designer TaVon Sneed, and cover designer Rosemary Murphy. Their attention to detail, creativity, and expertise ensured that this project was worthy for your use.

January 1

"Faith is taking the first step even when you don't see the whole staircase." ~ Dr. Martin Luther King Jr.

I have faith in my Creator, my community, and myself because...

_____

_____

_____

_____

_____

_____

_____

_____

_____

_____

_____

_____

_____

_____

_____

_____

_____

_____

Today is the seventh day of Kwanzaa, which celebrates the principal of Imani (Faith). We believe with all our heart in our Creator, ourselves, our people, and the righteousness and victory of our struggle.

I'm curious! Where was Kwanzaa first celebrated?

January 2

"Don't let anything stop you. There will be times when you'll be disappointed, but you can't stop. Make yourself the best that you can make out of what you are. The very best." ~ Sadie Alexander

I am unstoppable! I know I am unstoppable because...

_____

_____

_____

_____

_____

_____

_____

_____

_____

_____

_____

_____

_____

_____

_____

_____

_____

_____

Today in 1898, Sadie T.M. Alexander, was born in Philadelphia. She was the first African American woman to earn a Ph.D. in economics, the first to hold a Ph.D. and J.D., and the first to practice law in Philadelphia.

I'm curious! What organization was she the first national president of?

January 3

"Reaching deep down and finding confidence has made all my dreams come true." ~ Arsenio Hall

I have confidence that my dreams will come true because...

_____

_____

_____

_____

_____

_____

_____

_____

_____

_____

_____

_____

_____

_____

_____

_____

_____

_____

_____

Today in 1989, the Arsenio Hall Show premiered as the first regularly scheduled nightly talk show to star an African American. The show taped one thousand four hundred and six episodes and won two Emmys.

I'm curious! Who were other African American firsts on T.V.?

January 4

"If they don't give you a seat at the table, bring a folding chair."
~ Shirley Chisholm

I know that I belong at any table, even if I have to bring a chair, because...

_____

_____

_____

_____

_____

_____

_____

_____

_____

_____

_____

_____

_____

_____

_____

_____

_____

_____

Today in 1969, the Congressional Black Caucus was organized by U.S. House of Representatives to address the needs of African Americans including the right to quality housing and the eradication of racism.

I'm curious! What are the names of three of the thirteen organizers?

January 5

"He could have added fortune to fame, but caring for neither, he found happiness and honor in being helpful to the world."
~ Headstone of George Washington Carver

There are many ways that I can be helpful. I will be helpful to the world by

_____

_____

_____

_____

_____

_____

_____

_____

_____

_____

_____

_____

_____

_____

_____

_____

_____

Today is G.W. Carver Day named after the botanist and inventor who found hundreds of uses for everyday items. Born into slavery, he became a highly regarded professor at Tuskegee University in Alabama.

I'm curious! What were two of Dr. Carver's discoveries?

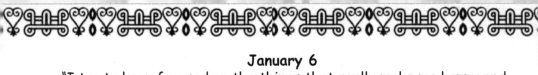

January 6
"I try to keep focused on the things that really make me happy and just do those same things." ~ John Singleton

I will focus on what makes me happy. A few things that make me happy are...

_____

_____

_____

_____

_____

_____

_____

_____

_____

_____

_____

_____

_____

_____

_____

_____

_____

_____

_____

Today in 1968, screenwriter, producer, and actor John Singleton was born in Los Angeles. He became the youngest person to ever be nominated for an Academy Award for Best Director at age twenty-four.

I'm curious! What movie was his nomination for?

January 7

"Those that don't got it, can't show it. Those that got it,
can't hide it."
~ Zora Neale Hurston

I got it and I can't hide it! I won't hide what I got because...

_____

_____

_____

_____

_____

_____

_____

_____

_____

_____

_____

_____

_____

_____

_____

_____

_____

_____

Today in 1891, Zora Neale Hurston was born. She wrote more than
fifty published short stories, plays, and essays. She is best known for
her 1937 novel, Their Eyes Were Watching God.

I'm curious! What town holds a yearly festival in her honor?

January 8

"Anytime anyone is enslaved, as far as I am concerned he is justified to resort to whatever methods necessary to bring about his liberty again." ~ Malcolm X

I will fight for my psychological liberty by...

_____

_____

_____

_____

_____

_____

_____

_____

_____

_____

_____

_____

_____

_____

_____

_____

_____

_____

_____

Today in 1811, the largest slave revolt in U.S. history occurred in what is now the state of Louisiana. Charles Deslondes, a slave born in Haiti, led the uprising.

I'm curious! Can you name another slave uprising?

January 9
"The Blacker the College, the Sweeter the Knowledge."
~ Unknown

For us, by us is important because...

_____

_____

_____

_____

_____

_____

_____

_____

_____

_____

_____

_____

_____

_____

_____

_____

_____

_____

_____

Today in 1866, Fisk University was established. Notable alumni include W.E.B. DuBois, Nikki Giovanni, and Marion Barry. Lincoln College in Missouri and Rust College in Mississippi were also established in 1866.

I'm curious! What famed traveling group raised money for Fisk?

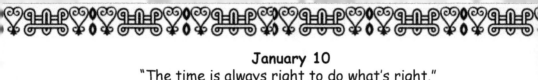

January 10
"The time is always right to do what's right."
~ Dr. Martin Luther King Jr.

I will do what's right for my community by...

_____
_____
_____
_____
_____
_____
_____
_____
_____
_____
_____
_____
_____
_____
_____
_____
_____
_____
_____

Today in 1957, The Southern Christian Leadership Conference (SCLC) was formed. Their purpose was to coordinate and support nonviolent, direct action as a method of desegregation.

I'm curious! What other initiatives were the SCLC involved in?

January 11

" [T]he slave went free; stood a brief moment in the sun; then moved back again toward slavery." ~ W.E.B. Du Bois

With faith and confidence, it is important that I stay in the sun because...

_____

_____

_____

_____

_____

_____

_____

_____

_____

_____

_____

_____

_____

_____

_____

_____

_____

_____

Today in 1870, the first Reconstruction legislature met in Jackson, Mississippi. Thirty-one of the one hundred and six representatives were Black. Five of the thirty-three senators were Black.

I'm curious! What was the Reconstruction era?

January 12

"The time is past when Christians in America can take a long spoon and hand the gospel to the black man out the back door."
~ Mordecai Johnson

I am coming to the front door because...

_____

_____

_____

_____

_____

_____

_____

_____

_____

_____

_____

_____

_____

_____

_____

_____

_____

_____

Today in 1890, Mordecai W. Johnson was born. He was the first Black president of Howard University and he is considered one of the three leading Black preachers of the early 20th century.

I'm curious! How long was Johnson the president of Howard?

January 13

"I could have never visualized something as powerful or as worthwhile." ~ Bertha Pitts Campbell-Delta Founder 1983

My powerful and worthwhile vision for myself is...

_____

_____

_____

_____

_____

_____

_____

_____

_____

_____

_____

_____

_____

_____

_____

_____

_____

_____

_____

Today in 1913, Delta Sigma Theta, Inc., the largest African American sorority was founded. It was established by twenty-two students at Howard and continues to be devoted to service and sisterhood.

I'm curious! What are some current Delta programs?

January 14

"There will be those who will tell you that you can't make it because of how you look, because of the way you talk. We all have heard that—I almost listened." ~Douglas Wilder

I am wonderfully made. I won't listen to negativity about myself because...

_____

_____

_____

_____

_____

_____

_____

_____

_____

_____

_____

_____

_____

_____

_____

_____

_____

_____

Today in 1990, Douglas Wilder became the first Black governor. He served Virginia in this role from 1990-1994. In 2005 he became the first Black-elected mayor of Richmond.

I'm curious! What other jobs did Douglas Wilder hold?

January 15
"No person has the right to rain on your dreams."
~ Dr. Martin Luther King Jr.

No amount of rain will stop my dreams! Today I am dreaming about...

_____

_____

_____

_____

_____

_____

_____

_____

_____

_____

_____

_____

_____

_____

_____

_____

_____

_____

Today in 1929, Dr. Martin Luther King Jr. was born in Atlanta. He would later become one of the most influential, recognizable civil rights leaders of all time.

I'm curious! What nonviolent leader was MLK's inspiration?

January 16

"Whether or not you reach your goals in life depends entirely on how well you prepare for them and how badly you want them."
~ Ronald McNair

I am preparing to reach my goals by...

_____

_____

_____

_____

_____

_____

_____

_____

_____

_____

_____

_____

_____

_____

_____

_____

_____

_____

Today in 1978, NASA named the first three
Black astronauts, Major Guion Stewart Bluford Jr.,
Major Frederick Drew Gregory, and Dr. Ronald McNair.

I'm curious! Who was the first Black female astronaut?

January 17

"A man who has no imagination has no wings."
~ Muhammad Ali

My imagination is limitless! I have wings and I will use them to...

_____

_____

_____

_____

_____

_____

_____

_____

_____

_____

_____

_____

_____

_____

_____

_____

_____

_____

Today in 1942, Muhammad Ali was born in Louisville, Kentucky. He would later become one of the greatest boxers and Black activists of all time.

I'm curious! Why didn't Ali fight from age twenty-five to almost twenty-nine?

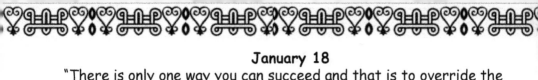

January 18

"There is only one way you can succeed and that is to override the
obstacles in your way by the power that is within you."
~ Dr. Daniel Hale Williams

I have superpowers! My superpowers are...

_____

_____

_____

_____

_____

_____

_____

_____

_____

_____

_____

_____

_____

_____

_____

_____

_____

_____

Today in 1856, Dr. Daniel Hale Williams was born. He performed
American's first successful open-heart surgery and also founded the
first non-segregated hospital in the US.

I'm curious! What was the name of his hospital?

January 19

"If you hold your hand closed, nothing good can come in. The open hand is blessed, for it gives in abundance, even as it receives."
~ Biddy Mason

As I have received so I will give...

_____

_____

_____

_____

_____

_____

_____

_____

_____

_____

_____

_____

_____

_____

_____

_____

_____

_____

Today in 1856, Bridgette "Biddy" Mason won the freedom of herself and thirteen members of her family in a Los Angeles court. She went on to buy land and establish the First Black Church in the city.

I'm curious! What was the name of her church?

January 20

"We did not come to fear the future. We came here to shape it."
~ with President Barack Obama

With my courage and my superpowers I will shape the future by...

_____

_____

_____

_____

_____

_____

_____

_____

_____

_____

_____

_____

_____

_____

_____

_____

_____

_____

_____

Today in 2009, President Barack Obama was sworn in as the first African American president of the United States of America. He previously served as a U.S. senator from 2005 to 2008.

I'm curious! What was his job after graduating from Columbia University?

January 21

"I'll leave here with my head held high and with confidence that history will judge my time here." ~ Eric Holder

I hold my head up high because...

_____

_____

_____

_____

_____

_____

_____

_____

_____

_____

_____

_____

_____

_____

_____

_____

_____

_____

Today in 1951, Eric H. Holder Jr. was born. He served as the first African American attorney general of the U.S. from 2009-2015. Previously, He served as a judge and U.S. attorney for the District of Columbia

I'm curious! Who was the Attorney General after Holder?

January 22

"It's been a long time coming, but I know, a change gonna come."
~ Sam Cooke

Racial injustice has existed since the birth of this country, but I will make a change by …

_____

_____

_____

_____

_____

_____

_____

_____

_____

_____

_____

_____

_____

_____

_____

_____

_____

Today in 1931, singer and activist Sam Cooke was born in Clarksdale, Mississippi and later raised in Chicago, Illinois. He joined his first singing group at age six and had 34 songs on the Billboard charts between 1958 and 1966.

I'm curious! Who were some of the other prominent people in his circle of friends?

January 23

"The way to succeed is never quit. That's it. But really be humble about it." ~ Alex Haley

I'll be humble and never quit because...

_____

_____

_____

_____

_____

_____

_____

_____

_____

_____

_____

_____

_____

_____

_____

_____

_____

_____

_____

Today in 1977, the miniseries Roots began airing on ABC. Based on the book written by Alex Haley, Roots was the most watched mini-series in history. In 1993, his miniseries, Queen, premiered.

I'm curious! What is the name of his bestselling book?

January 24
" Blacks have no history, heroes or accomplishments."
~ Arthur Schomburg's elementary teacher whom he proved wrong

I have history, heroes, and accomplishments! Some of my favorites heroes
are_____

_____

_____

_____

_____

_____

_____

_____

_____

_____

_____

_____

_____

_____

_____

_____

_____

Today in 1874, Arthur Schomburg was born. His collection of
literature, art, slave narratives, and other artifacts became the basis
of the Schomburg Center for Research in Black Culture.

I'm curious! How many pieces were in Schomburg's collection?

January 25
"I always worked. I was not afraid of getting my hands dirty."
~ Robert Johnson

I will work to accomplish...

_____

_____

_____

_____

_____

_____

_____

_____

_____

_____

_____

_____

_____

_____

_____

_____

_____

_____

_____

Today in 1980, Black Entertainment Television, known as BET, began broadcasting. It has grown to have several sister channels, newscasts, awards shows, and original programming.

I'm curious! Where does BET currently have offices?

January 26

"I am no longer accepting the things I cannot change. I am changing the things I cannot accept ~ Angela Davis

I am actively working to change the following things...

_____

_____

_____

_____

_____

_____

_____

_____

_____

_____

_____

_____

_____

_____

_____

_____

_____

_____

Today in 1944, social activist Dr. Angela Davis was born. Dr. Davis is a professor, researcher, and internationally recognized speaker. She has written several books on class, feminism, and the U.S. prison system.

I'm curious! In what tragedy were two of her childhood friends killed?

January 27

"When I discover who I am, I'll be free." ~ Ralph Ellison

To discover who I am I have to...

_____

_____

_____

_____

_____

_____

_____

_____

_____

_____

_____

_____

_____

_____

_____

_____

_____

_____

_____

Today in 1952, Ralph Ellison's Invisible Man wins the National Book Award. The novel explores an African American man's search for his identity and place in society in 1930s New York.

I'm curious! At what point of his life were his three later books published?

January 28

"The Lord was pleased to strengthen us, and remove all fear from us, and our hearts to be as useful as possible." ~ Richard Allen

With the strength of my Creator I will not fear...

_____

_____

_____

_____

_____

_____

_____

_____

_____

_____

_____

_____

_____

_____

_____

_____

_____

_____

_____

Today in 1787, the Free African Society was organized in Philadelphia by Richard Allen and Absalom Jones. FAS helped to establish independent Black churches and schools and provided medical care and social/economic guidance.

I'm curious! What denomination was FAS a precursor to?

January 29
"When I look into the future, it's so bright it burns my eyes."
~ Oprah Winfrey

My future is bright! In my future I see…

_____

_____

_____

_____

_____

_____

_____

_____

_____

_____

_____

_____

_____

_____

_____

_____

_____

_____

Today in 1954, Oprah Winfrey was born in Mississippi. Her television show was the highest rated show of its kind. She is a philanthropist, actress, producer, and the wealthiest African American of all time.

I'm curious! From which HBCU did Ms. Winfrey graduate?

January 30

"You may not have the power to change the world, but you can make a difference by creating an everlasting positive image."
~Herbert 'Flight Time' Lang

I will create a positive image! Reflecting on my image people will say...

_____

_____

_____

_____

_____

_____

_____

_____

_____

_____

_____

_____

_____

_____

_____

_____

_____

Today in 1927, the Harlem Globetrotters were formed. They have served as basketball's ambassadors of goodwill and have broken down many racial and cultural barriers throughout the years.

I'm curious! How many games and countries have they played?

January 31
"Don't agonize, organize." ~ Florynce Kennedy

I will organize to better my community because...

_____
_____
_____
_____
_____
_____
_____
_____
_____
_____
_____
_____
_____
_____
_____
_____
_____
_____

Today in 1961, the Civil Rights-era jail-in movement began when nine men from Rock Hill, South Carolina decided to serve thirty days in jail instead of paying $100 bail after being arrested for staging a lunch counter sit-in.

I'm curious! What was the nickname for this group of men?

February 1

"Hold fast to dreams, for if dreams die, life is a broken-winged bird that cannot fly." ~ Langston Hughes

Through faith, courage and hard work my dreams will not die! My dreams include...

_____

_____

_____

_____

_____

_____

_____

_____

_____

_____

_____

_____

_____

_____

_____

_____

_____

Today in 1901, poet Langston Hughes was born in Joplin, Missouri. He moved to New York City as a young man and wrote "jazz poetry." He was a leader of the Harlem Renaissance.

I'm curious! What was his role in the Civil Rights Movement?

February 2

"I thank the Association for the award, not so much for myself as for the students whom I represent." ~ Ernest E. Just

My loved ones have represented me, so I will represent...

_____

_____

_____

_____

_____

_____

_____

_____

_____

_____

_____

_____

_____

_____

_____

_____

_____

_____

_____

Today in 1915, biologist Ernest E. Just was the first recipient of the NAACP's Spingarn Medal for his research in fertilization and cell division. In 1996, a postage stamp was issued in his honor.

I'm curious! What fraternity did Dr. Just establish at Howard University?

February 3
"Ain't no man can avoid being born average, but there ain't no man got to be common." ~ Satchel Paige

I am far from common! The ways that I am uncommon include ...

_____
_____
_____
_____
_____
_____
_____
_____
_____
_____
_____
_____
_____
_____
_____
_____
_____
_____
_____

Today in 1920, the Negro Baseball League was formed. Thousands of Black players like Satchel Paige played in the league with teams and fans across the nation.

I'm curious! Which team was the last to disband?

February 4
"You can have an impact anywhere you are." ~ Tony Dungy

I will have an impact! My impact will be…

_____

_____

_____

_____

_____

_____

_____

_____

_____

_____

_____

_____

_____

_____

_____

_____

_____

_____

_____

Today in 2007, Tony Dungy became the first African American head coach to win the Super Bowl. He coached the Indiana Colts from 2002-2008 and the Tampa Buccaneers from 1996-2001.

I'm curious! What is the title of Coach Dungy's bestselling book?

February 5
"Failure is a part of success." ~ Hank Aaron

With perseverance, I will succeed at…

_____

_____

_____

_____

_____

_____

_____

_____

_____

_____

_____

_____

_____

_____

_____

_____

_____

_____

Today in 1934, baseball player Hank Aaron was born. He briefly
played in the Negro League and was the last Negro League baseball
player on a major league roster.

I'm curious! How many years did he play professional baseball?

February 6

"Don't worry about a thing, cause every little thing is gonna be all right." ~ Bob Marley

I won't worry because...

_____
_____
_____
_____
_____
_____
_____
_____
_____
_____
_____
_____
_____
_____
_____
_____
_____
_____
_____

Today in 1945, Jamaican reggae singer and Pan-Africanist Bob Marley was born. Some of his songs include "Buffalo Soldiers," "Redemption Song," and "One Love."

I'm curious! What are some of the things that he stood for?

February 7

"When you control a man's thinking you do not have to worry about his actions." ~ Carter G. Woodson

I will control my own thinking by...

_____

_____

_____

_____

_____

_____

_____

_____

_____

_____

_____

_____

_____

_____

_____

_____

_____

_____

_____

Today in 1926, Negro History Week, originated by Carter G. Woodson, is observed for the first time. The first observance of Black History Month was celebrated in 1970.

I'm curious! At what university was Black History Month celebrated in 1970?

February 8
" I will sink or swim with my race." ~ John S. Rock

My ancestors fought too hard for me to sink. In their honor I will swim and I will ...

_____

_____

_____

_____

_____

_____

_____

_____

_____

_____

_____

_____

_____

_____

_____

_____

_____

_____

Today in 1850, John S. Rock delivered a speech to white residents in New Jersey advocating for Blacks to have the right to vote. In 1865 he would become the first Black lawyer to argue a case before the Supreme Court.

I'm curious! What were his other three professions?

February 9
"You are an infinite being with infinite possibilities."
~ Dr. Bernard Harris

I will use my infinite possibilities to have an impact! It is possible for me to...

_____

_____

_____

_____

_____

_____

_____

_____

_____

_____

_____

_____

_____

_____

_____

_____

_____

_____

Today in 1995, astronaut and physician Dr. Bernard Harris became the first African American to perform a spacewalk. He was also involved in the construction of the space rovers.

I'm curious! Where is the middle school named in his honor?

February 10

"If a man can't go out in the blaze of glory, he can at least go with dignity." ~Nat Love

I am dignified! Being dignified means...

_____

_____

_____

_____

_____

_____

_____

_____

_____

_____

_____

_____

_____

_____

_____

_____

_____

_____

Today in 1869, Nat Love left his former slave plantation in Tennes see to head west at age sixteen. He became one of the most famous cowboys, Black or white, in history.

I'm curious! What did he title his autobiography published in 1907?

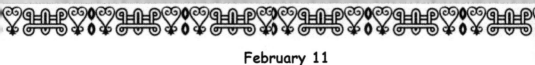

February 11
"Your playing small does not serve the world. Who are you not to be great?" ~ Nelson Mandela

I come from great people so I will be great! I will use my greatness to...

_____

_____

_____

_____

_____

_____

_____

_____

_____

_____

_____

_____

_____

_____

_____

_____

_____

Today in 1990, revolutionary and philanthropist Nelson Mandela was released from jail after being held as a political prisoner for twenty-seven years. Apartheid was eventually abolished in 1991.

I'm curious! When was Mandela elected as President?

February 12

"The way to right wrongs is to turn the light of truth upon them."
~ Ida B. Wells-Barnett

I am a light of truth! Being a light of truth means...

_____

_____

_____

_____

_____

_____

_____

_____

_____

_____

_____

_____

_____

_____

_____

_____

_____

_____

Today in 1909, the NAACP was founded. Their mission is to ensure the political, educational, social, and economic equality of rights of all persons and to eliminate racial hatred and discrimination.

I'm curious! What does the acronym NAACP stand for?

February 13

"The flowers absorb the sunshine because it is their nature. I give out melody because God filled my soul with it." ~ Sissieretta Jone

The Creator has given me so many gifts. Some of these gifts are...

_____

_____

_____

_____

_____

_____

_____

_____

_____

_____

_____

_____

_____

_____

_____

_____

_____

Today in 1893, opera singer Sissieretta Jones became the first Black artist to perform in Carnegie Hall's main auditorium. She was joined by the Fisk Jubilee Singers and Frederick Douglass.

I'm curious! What happened to her fortune?

February 14

"Just learn from your mistakes...and
forgive yourself...and better yourself." ~ Richard Allen

I've learned from my mistakes. I have learned that...

_____

_____

_____

_____

_____

_____

_____

_____

_____

_____

_____

_____

_____

_____

_____

_____

_____

Today in 1760, Richard Allen, founder of the African Methodist
Episcopal Church, was born into slavery in Philadelphia, Pennsylvania.
He was an abolitionist, educator, and one of the most influential Black
leaders in history.

I'm curious! In what year did he buy his freedom?

February 15

"It is very hard to retain self-respect if we see ourselves set apart
and avoided as a degraded race by others."
~ Attorney Robert Morris

I respect myself and others by...

_____

_____

_____

_____

_____

_____

_____

_____

_____

_____

_____

_____

_____

_____

_____

_____

_____

_____

Today in 1848, five-year-old Sarah Roberts was removed from her
school because she was Black. Her father sued the city and lost, but
paved the way for desegregation in Boston, Massachusetts.

I'm curious! What is the title of the 2004 book about Sarah?

February 16

"Zip-a-dee-doo-dah, zip-a-dee-ay. My oh my, what a wonderful day."
~ James Baskett (as "Uncle Remus")

Everyday that I wake up is a wonderful day. Today will be wonderful because...

_____

_____

_____

_____

_____

_____

_____

_____

_____

_____

_____

_____

_____

_____

_____

_____

_____

_____

Today in 1904, actor James Baskett was born. He became the first African American to win an Academy Award for his role as "Uncle Remus" in the Disney film Song of the South.

I'm curious! Why was he unable to attend the film's premiere?

February 17

"I have the people behind me and the people are my strength."
~ Huey P. Newton

I have people behind me! The people behind me are...

_____

_____

_____

_____

_____

_____

_____

_____

_____

_____

_____

_____

_____

_____

_____

_____

_____

_____

Today in 1942, activist Huey P. Newton was born. He and Bobby Seale co-founded the Black Panther Party to advocate for self-defense, while hosting social programs including Free Breakfast for Children.

I'm curious! What were some of the other social programs they started?

February 18

"If there's a book you really want to read, but it hasn't been written yet, then you must write it." ~ Toni Morrison

I will create what is missing because...

_____

_____

_____

_____

_____

_____

_____

_____

_____

_____

_____

_____

_____

_____

_____

_____

_____

_____

_____

Today in 1931, author Toni Morrison was born in Lorain, Ohio. She won a Pulitzer Prize for her novel Beloved. She is a Howard University alumna and won a Presidential Medal of Freedom.

I'm curious! What other major prize did she win?

February 19

"Aim high, believe in yourself, use your brain, never quit, be ready to go, expect to win." ~ The Tuskegee Airmen

I believe in myself just as my community believes in me. My guiding principles are...

_____

_____

_____

_____

_____

_____

_____

_____

_____

_____

_____

_____

_____

_____

_____

_____

_____

_____

Today in 1942, the Tuskegee Airmen were initiated into the Armed Forces. They flew over seven hundred bomber escort missions and were the only fighters to have a perfect protection record.

I'm curious! How many pilots graduated from the program?

February 20

"I am the me I choose to be." ~ Sidney Poitier

I am unique and serve a specific purpose in this world. I choose to be...

_____

_____

_____

_____

_____

_____

_____

_____

_____

_____

_____

_____

_____

_____

_____

_____

_____

_____

Today in 1927, actor Sidney Poitier was born. He was the first Black person to be awarded an Academy Award for Best Actor. He also served as the Bahamian ambassador to Japan.

I'm curious! What medal did he receive in 2009?

February 21

"I'll tell you what freedom is to me: no fear. I mean really, no fear!"
~ Nina Simone

I won't fear because...

_____
_____
_____
_____
_____
_____
_____
_____
_____
_____
_____
_____
_____
_____
_____
_____
_____
_____

Today in 1933, singer-songwriter and pianist Nina Simone was born in Tyron, North Carolina. She recorded more than forty albums and was also an activist in the Civil Rights Movement.

I'm curious! What activist did she live next door to in New York City?

February 22
"There's no need to argue, parents just don't understand."
~ DJ Jazzy Jeff and the Fresh Prince

I need my parents to understand that I…

_____

_____

_____

_____

_____

_____

_____

_____

_____

_____

_____

_____

_____

_____

_____

_____

_____

_____

Today in 1989, DJ Jazzy Jeff and the Fresh Prince won the first
Grammy Award for Best Rap Performance for the song "Parents Just
Don't Understand." They have sold over 5.5 million albums in the U.S.

I'm curious! For what song did the group earn their second Grammy?

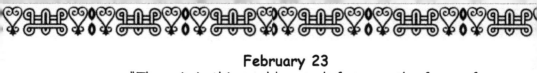

February 23

"There is in this world no such force as the force of a person determined to rise." ~ W.E.B. Du Bois

I will rise to...

_____

_____

_____

_____

_____

_____

_____

_____

_____

_____

_____

_____

_____

_____

_____

_____

_____

_____

Today in 1868, W.E.B. Du Bois, activist and historian, was born in Great Barrington, Massachusetts. He was the first African American to earn a Ph.D. from Harvard University and he authored The Souls of Black Folk.

I'm curious! What organization did he co-found?

February 24

"When God has a work to be executed he also chooses the man to execute it. He also qualifies the workman for the work." ~ Bishop Daniel Payne

I have been chosen to...

_____

_____

_____

_____

_____

_____

_____

_____

_____

_____

_____

_____

_____

_____

_____

_____

_____

_____

_____

Today in 1811, Daniel Payne was born. He helped shape the AME Church and was a founder of Wilberforce University, where he served as the first Black university president in history.

I'm curious! What school is named in his honor?

February 25

Don't count the days, make the days count." ~ Muhammad Ali

I will make today count by...

_____
_____
_____
_____
_____
_____
_____
_____
_____
_____
_____
_____
_____
_____
_____
_____
_____
_____

Today in 1964, what has been regarded as one of the greatest sporting events of all time took place. Muhammad Ali won the World Boxing Heavyweight Championship, defeating Sonny Liston in a seventh- round knockout.

I'm curious! What boxer won the Championship on this day in 1989?

February 26
"An experience of a lifetime." ~ Camp Atwater

I will create fulfilling experiences by...

_____

_____

_____

_____

_____

_____

_____

_____

_____

_____

_____

_____

_____

_____

_____

_____

_____

_____

Today in 1921, Camp Atwater was founded in North Brookfield, Massachusetts. It is the oldest accredited African American camp in the nation, focusing on culture, education, and recreation.

I'm curious! What camp for Black girls was founded in 1924?

February 27

"Her admission to the bar was secured by a clever ruse, her name being sent in with her classmates as C.E. Ray ~ L.J. Robinson

My ancestors have always been clever. I can be just as clever when..

_____

_____

_____

_____

_____

_____

_____

_____

_____

_____

_____

_____

_____

_____

_____

_____

_____

_____

Today in 1872, Charlotte E. Ray became the first Black female attorney in the U.S. She graduated from Howard University School of Law and became the first female to be admitted to the D.C. Bar.

I'm curious! What was she also the first woman to do?

February 28

"You can't hurt me, I found peace within myself."
~ Michael Jackson

To me, having inner peace means....

_____

_____

_____

_____

_____

_____

_____

_____

_____

_____

_____

_____

_____

_____

_____

_____

_____

_____

Today in 1984, Michael Jackson won eight Grammys, the most ever won in one night at that time. Album of the Year Thriller was the world's best-selling record and was produced by Quincy Jones.

I'm curious! How many of the eight songs did he write?

February 29
I did my best, and God did the rest." ~Hattie McDaniel

With my creator's help I'll do my best to...

_____
_____
_____
_____
_____
_____
_____
_____
_____
_____
_____
_____
_____
_____
_____
_____
_____
_____

Today in 1940, actress Hattie McDaniel became the first Black Oscar winner for her role as "Mammy" in the film Gone With the Wind. She was also the first Black woman to sing on radio in the U.S.

I'm curious! In approximately how many movies did she appear?

March 1

"You can cage the singer but not the song." ~ Harry Belafonte

My song will not be caged! I will sing so people can hear me because ...

_____

_____

_____

_____

_____

_____

_____

_____

_____

_____

_____

_____

_____

_____

_____

_____

_____

_____

Today in 1927, Harry Belafonte, entertainer and social activist, was born. He served as one of Dr. King's confidants and was an advocate for civil, political, and humanitarian rights.

I'm curious! Which of his albums was the first million seller ever?

March 2

"I just couldn't move. History had me glued to the seat."
~ Claudette Colvin

I am unmovable in my belief that...

_____

_____

_____

_____

_____

_____

_____

_____

_____

_____

_____

_____

_____

_____

_____

_____

_____

_____

Today in 1955, Claudette Colvin refused to give up her seat on a bus, nine months before Rosa Parks. She was arrested for disturbing the peace and later became a plaintiff in a case which determined that segregation was illegal.

I'm curious! Why was Colvin not chosen as the face of the Montgomery Bus Boycott?

March 3

"Jennings was 'a bold man of color' who led an 'active, earnest and blameless life.'" ~ Frederick Douglass

I am bold! I demonstrated my boldness when...

_____

_____

_____

_____

_____

_____

_____

_____

_____

_____

_____

_____

_____

_____

_____

_____

_____

_____

Today in 1821, abolitionist and tailor Thomas L. Jennings was the first African American to receive a patent, inventing a new dry cleaning process. With his proceeds, he bought his family's freedom.

I'm curious! What famous church did he found in Harlem, New York?

March 4

"If you want to do something then be the best."
~ Garrett Morgan

If I'm going to do something, I'm going to do it to the best of my ability! I will be the best at ...

_____

_____

_____

_____

_____

_____

_____

_____

_____

_____

_____

_____

_____

_____

_____

_____

Today in 1877, inventor and entrepreneur Garrett Morgan was born in Paris, Kentucky. He is most famous for inventing hair care products, a smoke protection safety hood, and the traffic signal.

I'm curious! What group did he help found in 1908?

March 5

"First man to die for the flag we now hold high was a Black man."
~ Stevie Wonder—Black Man (1976)

I will sacrifice for what I believe in. I strongly believe ...

_____

_____

_____

_____

_____

_____

_____

_____

_____

_____

_____

_____

_____

_____

_____

_____

_____

_____

Today in 1770, Crispus Attucks became the first American killed in the Revolutionary War. His death was used to demonstrate the significance of Black citizens and our sacrifices for a country that enslaved us.

I'm curious! What are some ways that his life has been memorialized?

March 6

"When you know more, you can do more." ~ Marion Barry

My ancestors did a lot and I can do more! I will do more to...

_____
_____
_____
_____
_____
_____
_____
_____
_____
_____
_____
_____
_____
_____
_____
_____

Today in 1936, Mayor Marion S. Barry was born in Mississippi. He served as the second mayor of the District of Columbia and then again as the fourth, becoming the first prominent civil rights activist to lead a major city.

I'm curious! How has he been memorialized in Washington, D.C.?

March 7

"You cannot be afraid to speak up for what you believe. You have to have courage, raw courage." ~ John Lewis

I am courageous when I...

_____

_____

_____

_____

_____

_____

_____

_____

_____

_____

_____

_____

_____

_____

_____

_____

_____

_____

Today in 1965, activists began their march from Selma to Montgomery, Alabama to advocate for voting rights. The nonviolent protesters were attacked by whites and the day became known as Bloody Sunday.

I'm curious! When was the march finally completed?

March 8

"There's one thing I don't ever think about: losing... Instead, I think about how I'm going to win" ~ Joe Frazier

I am a winner! Here are all the ways I'm winning ...

_____

_____

_____

_____

_____

_____

_____

_____

_____

_____

_____

_____

_____

_____

_____

_____

_____

_____

Today in 1971, the "Fight of the Century" occurred at Madison Square Garden with two undefeated champions, Muhammad Ali (31-0, 25 Knock Outs) and Joe Frazier (26-0, 23 Knock Outs).

I'm curious! Who won the fight?

March 9

"And before I'd be a slave I'll be buried in my grave, and go home to my Lord and be free" ~ "Oh, Freedom"

Freedom is important to me because ...

_____

_____

_____

_____

_____

_____

_____

_____

_____

_____

_____

_____

_____

_____

_____

_____

_____

_____

_____

Today in 1841, SCOTUS decided that illegally enslaved Africans who arrived on the Amistad ship be returned to Africa. It has been described as one of the most important cases involving slavery.

I'm curious! What criminal charges did they face for their revolt?

March 10

"Don't ever stop. Keep going." ~ Harriet Tubman

I won't stop trying and believing that ...

_____

_____

_____

_____

_____

_____

_____

_____

_____

_____

_____

_____

_____

_____

_____

_____

_____

Today is Harriet Tubman Day during which she is celebrated for being an abolitionist and political activist who made at least thirteen missions to rescue approximately seventy enslaved people.

I'm curious! What were some of her other jobs throughout her life?

March 11
"But let the record show we ain't going to be turned around."
~ Ralph Abernathy

Throughout history, Black people have been steadfast. I must go forward in my goal to ...

_____

_____

_____

_____

_____

_____

_____

_____

_____

_____

_____

_____

_____

_____

_____

_____

_____

_____

Today in 1926, civil rights activist Ralph Abernathy was born in Linden, Alabama. He and Dr. King collaborated on the Montgomery Bus Boycott and to form the Southern Christian Leadership Conference.

I'm curious! What campaign did he lead in 1968?

March 12

"Evil communication corrupts good manners." ~ Benjamin Banneker

I am mindful of how I speak to others. Being mindful when I speak to others means ...

_____

_____

_____

_____

_____

_____

_____

_____

_____

_____

_____

_____

_____

_____

_____

_____

_____

_____

_____

Today in 1791, Benjamin Banneker was commissioned to create the original borders for Washington, D.C. He was a self-taught almanac author, surveyor, mathematician, and astronomer.

I'm curious! What happened to his papers and belongings in 1806?

March 13

"His character was such that Native Americans petitioned to have
him named as the administrator of their affairs"
~ U.S. Postal Service

The characteristics of a good and important character are …

_____

_____

_____

_____

_____

_____

_____

_____

_____

_____

_____

_____

_____

_____

_____

_____

_____

_____

Today in 1773, explorer Jean Baptiste Point du Sable established the
first permanent settlement in what is now known as Chicago, Illinois.
He was also a trader, merchant, and operator of a river ferry.

I'm curious! Where is the museum that is named in his honor?

March 14

"Once a task is just begun, never leave it till it's done. Be the labor great or small, do it well or not at all." ~ Quincy Jones

Sometimes things are hard, but I have support and the will to push through. Things I do well include ...

_____

_____

_____

_____

_____

_____

_____

_____

_____

_____

_____

_____

_____

_____

_____

_____

_____

_____

Today in 1933, musician Quincy Jones was born in Chicago, Illinois. He produced The Wiz soundtrack in 1978 and co-produced three of Michael Jackson's albums. He has eighty Grammy nominations and won twenty- eight.

I'm curious! Which of his songs was played during the 1969 moon landing?

March 15

"Don't spend where you can't work." ~ Leon Washington Jr.

Black representation and Black buying power is important to our people. I will use my financial resources wisely because …

_____

_____

_____

_____

_____

_____

_____

_____

_____

_____

_____

_____

_____

_____

_____

_____

_____

_____

Today in 1933, the oldest, largest, and most influential newspaper on the West Coast was established. The Los Angeles Sentinel was founded by Leon Washington Jr.

I'm curious! Who edited and published the paper until 1990?

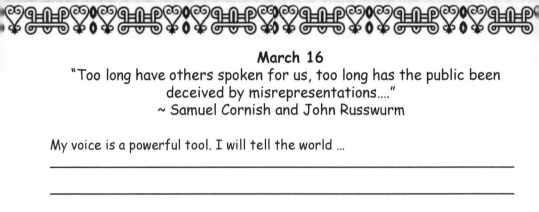

March 16

"Too long have others spoken for us, too long has the public been deceived by misrepresentations...."
~ Samuel Cornish and John Russwurm

My voice is a powerful tool. I will tell the world ...

_____

_____

_____

_____

_____

_____

_____

_____

_____

_____

_____

_____

_____

_____

_____

_____

_____

_____

Today in 1827, the first Black owned and operated newspaper, Freedom's Journal, was established. Its mission was to oppose newspapers that attacked Blacks and encouraged slavery.

I'm curious! Where was the paper circulated?

March 17

"I have had the desire to prove people wrong, to show I could do things they didn't think I could." ~ David Paterson

Because I believe in myself I know that I will ...

_____

_____

_____

_____

_____

_____

_____

_____

_____

_____

_____

_____

_____

_____

_____

_____

_____

_____

_____

Today in 2008, David A. Paterson was sworn in as the first African American governor of New York. He was also the first minority leader of the New York Senate.

I'm curious! What was his disability?

March 18

"Success is the sweetest revenge." ~ Vanessa L. Williams

I don't need to seek revenge. Instead I will …

_____

_____

_____

_____

_____

_____

_____

_____

_____

_____

_____

_____

_____

_____

_____

_____

_____

_____

Today in 1963, actress, singer, and designer Vanessa L. Williams was born in New York City, New York. In 1983, she became the first Black woman to be crowned Miss America. She has starred on television, film, and Broadway.

I'm curious! For what role did she receive a NAACP Image Award?

March 19

"Through his dedication and perseverance, Parsons prospered in various roles." ~ Jessie Carney Smith

I am dedicated to...

_____

_____

_____

_____

_____

_____

_____

_____

_____

_____

_____

_____

_____

_____

_____

_____

_____

_____

_____

Today in 1975, James B. Parsons becomes the first Black chief judge of a federal court, the U.S. District Court of Chicago. In 1961, he was the first African American to serve as a federal judge.

I'm curious! What was his first career?

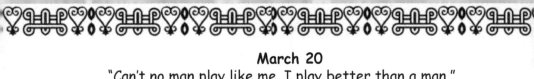

March 20

"Can't no man play like me. I play better than a man."
~ Sister Rosetta

I will not be limited! I will put all my potential to use because ...

_____

_____

_____

_____

_____

_____

_____

_____

_____

_____

_____

_____

_____

_____

_____

_____

_____

_____

Today in 1915, singer-songwriter Rosetta Tharpe was born. She was the first popular gospel recording star and the first to appeal to R& B and rock and roll audiences.

I'm curious! What nickname is used to reference her impact?

March 21

"You can never know where you are going unless you know where you have been." ~ Amelia Boynton

I know where I'm going. I am going to ...

_____

_____

_____

_____

_____

_____

_____

_____

_____

_____

_____

_____

_____

_____

_____

_____

_____

_____

_____

Today in 1965, protesters calling for voting rights started the third march from Selma to Montgomery. The fifty-four mile march was led by Dr. King and was joined by twenty-five thousand people.

"I'm curious! What happened during the previous two marches?

March 22

"He was a pioneer playing the leadership, authority and
intellectual position of quarterback." ~ Harry Edwards

I demonstrate leadership, authority and intellect daily by ...

_____

_____

_____

_____

_____

_____

_____

_____

_____

_____

_____

_____

_____

_____

_____

_____

_____

_____

Today in 1930, football player Willie Thrower was born in New
Kennsington, Pennsylvania. He played at Michigan State and was the
first African American quarterback in the Big Ten. He also played in
the NFL as a member of the Chicago Bears.

I'm curious! How was he impacted by racism in school?

March 23

"The only thing that matters is that you set a goal and you just dream, live, and fly." ~ Barrington Irving Jr.

To accomplish my goals I must ...

_____

_____

_____

_____

_____

_____

_____

_____

_____

_____

_____

_____

_____

_____

_____

_____

_____

_____

_____

Today in 2007, Barrington Irving Jr. became the youngest and first Black person to pilot a plane around the world solo. His plane was assembled using over $300,000 in donated parts.

I'm curious! What was the name of his plane?

March 24

"Without community service we wouldn't have a strong quality of life."
~ Dorothy Height

I serve my community by ...

_____

_____

_____

_____

_____

_____

_____

_____

_____

_____

_____

_____

_____

_____

_____

_____

_____

Today in 1912, Dorothy I. Height was born in Richmond, Virginia. She served as the tenth national president of Delta Sigma Theta Sorority and was the president of the National Council of Negro Women for forty years.

I'm curious! Who was her mentor?

March 25

"Sometimes, what you're looking for is already there."
~ Aretha Franklin

I am here and I am present. To be fully present means ...

_____

_____

_____

_____

_____

_____

_____

_____

_____

_____

_____

_____

_____

_____

_____

_____

_____

_____

Today in 1942, Aretha Franklin was born. She was a singer,
songwriter, civil rights activist, and pianist. She won eighteen
Grammy Awards and lived most of her life in Detroit.

I'm curious! What award did she win eight times in a row?

March 26

"I can be a better me than anyone can." ~ Diana Ross

I am the best me when...

_____

_____

_____

_____

_____

_____

_____

_____

_____

_____

_____

_____

_____

_____

_____

_____

_____

Today in 1944, Diana Ross was born in Detroit. She was the lead singer of the Supremes, Motown's most successful act. She also starred in the movies The Wiz, Mahogany, and Lady Sings the Blues.

I'm curious! Why is she in the Guinness Book of World Records?

March 27

"Let's all sit together as human beings should." ~ Unknown

My humanity cannot be questioned because...

_____

_____

_____

_____

_____

_____

_____

_____

_____

_____

_____

_____

_____

_____

_____

_____

_____

_____

_____

Today in 1867, the first recorded sit-in occurred. Demonstrators in Charleston, South Carolina staged ride-ins on streetcars. Although it was against the rules, many got on and refused to get back off.

I'm curious! When were the streetcar rules finally changed?

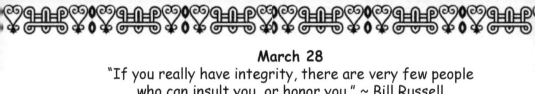

March 28

"If you really have integrity, there are very few people
who can insult you, or honor you." ~ Bill Russell

I have integrity and I demonstrate it when I...

_____

_____

_____

_____

_____

_____

_____

_____

_____

_____

_____

_____

_____

_____

_____

_____

_____

_____

Today in 1966, Bill Russell was named the head coach of the Boston
Celtics, making him the first African American NBA coach. As a
player, he won an Olympic gold medal and eleven NBA championships.

I'm curious! In childhood, what was his most prized possession?

March 29

"The star must slay his ego and learn teamwork and communication before he can achieve the ultimate in sport" ~ Walt Frazier

I am a communicator and a team player. I show this by...

_____

_____

_____

_____

_____

_____

_____

_____

_____

_____

_____

_____

_____

_____

_____

_____

_____

_____

_____

Today in 1945, broadcaster, former basketball player and fashion icon Walter "Clyde" Frazier was born in Atlanta. He won two NBA championships and was inducted into the Basketball Hall of Fame.

I'm curious! What line of tennis shoes were named after him?

March 30
"I'm sick and tired of being sick and tired." ~ Fannie Lou Hamer

Just like my voice is a powerful tool, so is my vote. My vote will have the power to...

_____

_____

_____

_____

_____

_____

_____

_____

_____

_____

_____

_____

_____

_____

_____

_____

_____

_____

Today in 1870, the Fifteenth Amendment was ratified prohibiting denying citizens the right to vote based on color or previous enslavement. Unfortunately, we continue to fight against voter suppression.

I'm curious! Who are three leaders who have fought for voters' rights?

March 31

"You are your best thing." ~ Toni Morrison, Beloved

I am my best thing! Things I love about myself include...

_____

_____

_____

_____

_____

_____

_____

_____

_____

_____

_____

_____

_____

_____

_____

_____

_____

Today in 1988, author, editor and professor, Toni Morrison won a Pulitzer Prize for her novel Beloved. The story is about two women who escape slavery but live in a haunted house.

I'm curious! Who starred in the movie adaptation of Beloved.

April 1

"Father Tolton encountered mistreatment and hate with faith, hope, and love. He persevered even when there seemed to be no logical reason to do so." ~ Bishop Joseph Perry

With faith, hope, love for myself and love from my community I can persevere. I want to persevere at...

_____

_____

_____

_____

_____

_____

_____

_____

_____

_____

_____

_____

_____

_____

_____

_____

_____

_____

Today in in 1854, Augustus Tolton became the first African American Roman Catholic priest in the U.S. He was a former slave and later formally studied in Rome, Italy.

I'm curious! How old was he when he was ordained?

April 2
"War is not the answer, because only love can conquer hate."
~ Marvin Gaye

Love can conquer hate! I have love in my heart and with that love I can...

_____

_____

_____

_____

_____

_____

_____

_____

_____

_____

_____

_____

_____

_____

_____

_____

_____

Today in 1939, songwriter Marvin Gaye was born in Washington, D.C. He helped to shape the sound of Motown in the 1960s and wrote songs that included "Inner City Blues" and "Pride and Joy."

I'm curious! What was his last live, now legendary, TV performance?

April 3

"We mean business now and we are determined to gain our rightful place in God's world." ~ Dr. Martin Luther King Jr.

With my rightful place in the world I will...

_____

_____

_____

_____

_____

_____

_____

_____

_____

_____

_____

_____

_____

_____

_____

_____

_____

_____

Today in 1968, Dr. Martin Luther King Jr. delivered his last speech "I've Been to the Mountaintop." He called for unity and economic actions, while challenging the U.S. to live up to its ideals.

I'm curious! The speech primarily concerns what strike?

April 4

"If Jesus was called to preach the Gospel to the poor, Martin Luther was called to give dignity to the common man." ~ Dr. Benjamin E. Mays

I have faith, purpose and dignity. With my dignity I can...

_____

_____

_____

_____

_____

_____

_____

_____

_____

_____

_____

_____

_____

_____

_____

_____

_____

_____

Today in 1968, Dr. Martin Luther King Jr. was assassinated. Heartbroken and frustrated by the death of a Civil Rights leader committed to peace, a nationwide wave of riots erupted in nearly 100 cities.

I'm curious! How many people took part in the funeral processional?

April 5
"If you want to lift yourself up, lift up someone else."
~ Booker T. Washington

I lift up others by...

_____

_____

_____

_____

_____

_____

_____

_____

_____

_____

_____

_____

_____

_____

_____

_____

_____

Today in 1856, educator, orator, presidential advisor, and Tuskegee University founder Booker T. Washington was born into slavery. He advocated for the empowerment of Blacks through education and entrepreneurship.

I'm curious! How old was he when he became the leader of Tuskegee?

April 6

"The great accomplishments of the world have been achieved by men who had high ideals and who have received great visions."
~ Matthew Henson

I have high ideals! I envision...

_____

_____

_____

_____

_____

_____

_____

_____

_____

_____

_____

_____

_____

_____

_____

_____

_____

_____

_____

Today in 1909, explorer and navigator Matthew Henson became the first man to reach the geographic North Pole. Born in Nanjemoy, Maryland to sharecropper parents, he spent over twenty-three years on expeditions.

I'm curious! What was the title of his memoir?

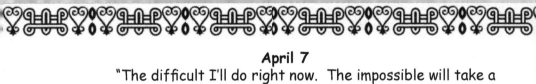

April 7

"The difficult I'll do right now. The impossible will take a little while." ~ Billie Holiday

I have confidence in myself. I know that I can ...

_____

_____

_____

_____

_____

_____

_____

_____

_____

_____

_____

_____

_____

_____

_____

_____

_____

_____

Today in 1915, influential jazz singer Billie Holiday was born in Baltimore. She sold out concerts in Carnegie Hall and on Broadway despite facing serious adversities.

I'm curious! Who played her in the 1972 movie about her life?

April 8

"All business is persona l.... Make your friends before you need them."
~ Robert Johnson

I value my friends. Some characteristics of a healthy friendship include ...

_____

_____

_____

_____

_____

_____

_____

_____

_____

_____

_____

_____

_____

_____

_____

_____

_____

_____

Today in 1946, BET Networks Co-Founder Robert L. Johnson was born in Hickory, Mississippi. He became the first Black American billionaire and was the first African American majority owner of a major sports team.

I'm curious! What was the name of his team?

April 9

"If you have a purpose in which you can believe, there's no end to the amount of things you can accomplish." ~ Marion Anderson

I believe in myself and I know that I can accomplish what I believe in! I want to accomplish ...

_____

_____

_____

_____

_____

_____

_____

_____

_____

_____

_____

_____

_____

_____

_____

_____

_____

_____

Today in 1939, Marion Anderson performed for seventy-five thousand people on the steps of the Lincoln Memorial. This concert occurred after she was refused permission to sing at Constitution Hall because she was Black.

I'm curious! In 1955, where was Marion Anderson the first Black person to perform?

April 10

"The bands of bondage were so strong that no way appeared for my release: yet at times a hope arose in my heart that a way would open for it." ~ Bishop Richard Allen

Hope arises in my heart that I can...

_____

_____

_____

_____

_____

_____

_____

_____

_____

_____

_____

_____

_____

_____

_____

_____

_____

_____

_____

Today in 1816 Richard Allen was elected as the first bishop of the AME church. Bishop Allen was born enslaved but bought his freedom and became a minister, educator, writer, and leader.

I'm curious! Who was his wife?

April 11

"The ultimate expression of generosity is not in giving of what you have, but in giving of who you are." ~ Johnetta B. Cole

I give of who I am by...

_____

_____

_____

_____

_____

_____

_____

_____

_____

_____

_____

_____

_____

_____

_____

_____

_____

_____

Today in 1881, Spelman College opened in the basement of a Baptist Church. Spelman has been ranked first among HBCUs and is the second largest producer of African American graduates who attend medical school.

I'm curious! Who was Spelman's first African American president?

April 12

"But, the truth is that everyone is somebody already." ~ Herbie Hancock

I descend from a lot of somebodies. I am...

_____

_____

_____

_____

_____

_____

_____

_____

_____

_____

_____

_____

_____

_____

_____

_____

_____

Today in 1940, jazz musician Herbie Hancock was born in Chicago, Illinois. He has played with the Miles Davis Quintet and has the second jazz album that won the Grammy for Album of the Year.

I'm curious! What cartoon did he compose the soundtrack for?

April 13

"The greatest thing about tomorrow is I will be better than I am today." ~Tiger Woods

Today I am great! Tomorrow will be better because ...

_____

_____

_____

_____

_____

_____

_____

_____

_____

_____

_____

_____

_____

_____

_____

_____

_____

_____

Today in 1997, twenty-one-year-old Tiger Woods won the Professional Golf Association's (PGA) Masters Tournament. He was the first African American and youngest player to do so. He is regarded as one of the most famous athletes and greatest golfers of all time.

I'm curious! How old was he when he played golf on television for the first time?

April 14

"Each generation has a critical responsibility help provide the shoulders, the direction, and the support for those generations who come behind." ~ Dr. Gloria Randle Scott

I will help those who come behind me by...

_____

_____

_____

_____

_____

_____

_____

_____

_____

_____

_____

_____

_____

_____

_____

_____

_____

_____

_____

Today in 1938, educator Dr. Gloria Randle Scott was born in Houston, Texas. She was the first African American president of Girl Scouts and also served as the president of Bennett College in Greensboro, North Carolina.

I'm curious! What type of school is Bennett College?

April 15

"I want to be a mayor who helped, really helped."
~ Harold Washington

I want to help, really help with …

_____

_____

_____

_____

_____

_____

_____

_____

_____

_____

_____

_____

_____

_____

_____

_____

_____

_____

Today in 1922, politician Harold Washington was born. He became the first African American to be elected as mayor of Chicago, Illinois. He served from 1983 to his death in 1987.

I'm curious! Why did he drop out of high school?

April 16

"[A]ll persons held to service or labor within D.C. by reason of African descent are hereby discharged and freed of and from all claim to such service or labor" ~ D.C. Emancipation Act

I am free! I will use my freedom to ...

_____

_____

_____

_____

_____

_____

_____

_____

_____

_____

_____

_____

_____

_____

_____

_____

_____

_____

Today in 1862, Abraham Lincoln signed an act that ended slavery in Washington, D.C. by paying white enslavers for releasing those they enslaved, three years before slavery was ended throughout the U.S.

I'm curious! What amendment ended legal slavery?

April 17
"Have a belief in yourself that is bigger than anyone's disbelief." ~ August Wilson

I believe in myself! I believe that I will...

_____

_____

_____

_____

_____

_____

_____

_____

_____

_____

_____

_____

_____

_____

_____

_____

_____

_____

Today in 1990, August Wilson's play, The Piano Lesson, received the Pulitzer Prize for Drama. The play is set in 1936 Pittsburg, Pennsylvania and focuses on a family's disagreements about their legacy.

I'm curious! When did the play make it to Broadway?

April 18

"The grave of Nick Biddle a Mecca should be /To Pilgrims, who seek in this land of the free." ~ James M. Guthrie

I remember those who have sacrificed for me because...

_____
_____
_____
_____
_____
_____
_____
_____
_____
_____
_____
_____
_____
_____
_____
_____
_____
_____
_____

Today in 1861, former slave Nicholas Biddle was the first soldier wounded in the Civil War. President Lincoln suggested Biddle seek treatment after being hit in the head with a brick, but he decided to stay with the troops.

I'm curious! How old was he when he was wounded?

April 19

"I'd be happy to play on the team if the rules were not structured against me and my people." ~ Max Robinson

I am a team player when the rules are fair. Being a team player means ...

_____

_____

_____

_____

_____

_____

_____

_____

_____

_____

_____

_____

_____

_____

_____

_____

_____

_____

Today in 1978, journalist Max Robinson became the first African American broadcast network news anchor in the U.S. He was also a founder of the Association of Black Journalists.

I'm curious! What is the mission of the center named in his honor?

April 20

"Always remember, you have within you the strength, the patience, and the passion to reach for the stars to change the world."
~ Harriet Tubman

I have strength, patience, and passion and I will use these things to change the world by...

_____

_____

_____

_____

_____

_____

_____

_____

_____

_____

_____

_____

_____

_____

_____

_____

_____

_____

Today in 1853, abolitionist and suffrage activist Harriet Tubman began her work with the Underground Railroad. It is estimated that she made thirteen trips and escorted about seventy enslaved people to the North.

I'm curious! Whom did she escort on her first trip with "passengers."

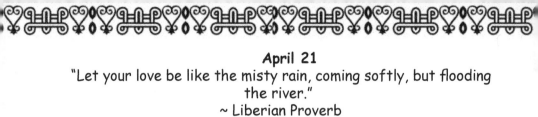

April 21

"Let your love be like the misty rain, coming softly, but flooding the river."
~ Liberian Proverb

My love for my people floods rivers. A few things about my people that I love are

_____

_____

_____

_____

_____

_____

_____

_____

_____

_____

_____

_____

_____

_____

_____

_____

Today in 1878, a bark called the Azor set sail with two hundred and six Black people from South Carolina to Liberia. Those who joined the Liberian exodus were seeking to leave the injustices they suffered in the U.S. for a better life in Africa.

I'm curious! What congressman and AME minister led this movement?

April 22

"Nearly 100 enslaved men and women beat drums and marched in unison with a banner marked 'Liberty' chanting 'Lukango' liberty in Kongolese."
~ National Museum of African American History and Culture

I imagine that to the slave "liberty" meant...

_____

_____

_____

_____

_____

_____

_____

_____

_____

_____

_____

_____

_____

_____

_____

_____

_____

_____

_____

Today in 1596, the first recorded slave revolt occurred in Stono, South Carolina. There is documented evidence of more than two hundred and fifty uprisings including those led by Gabriel Prosser and Denmark Vesey.

I'm curious! Who led the most famous uprising of all?

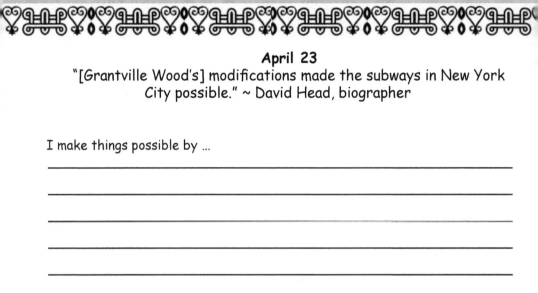

April 23

"[Grantville Wood's] modifications made the subways in New York City possible." ~ David Head, biographer

I make things possible by ...

_____

_____

_____

_____

_____

_____

_____

_____

_____

_____

_____

_____

_____

_____

_____

_____

_____

_____

Today in 1856, inventor Granville Woods was born in Columbus, Ohio. He held more than fifty patents and was the first African American to be a mechanical and electrical engineer.

I'm curious! On what did most of his work focus?

April 24

"He would come into a field that had been well studied and find something really new that was remarkable." ~ Thomas Ferguson

I am remarkable in so many ways! A few of those ways include...

_____
_____
_____
_____
_____
_____
_____
_____
_____
_____
_____
_____
_____
_____
_____
_____
_____
_____
_____

Today in 1919, mathematician David Blackwell was born in Centralia, Illinois. He was the first African American inducted into the National Academy of Sciences and the seventh to receive a PhD in mathematics.

I'm curious! At which HBCUs did he teach?

April 25
"A mind is a terrible thing to waste."
~ United Negro College Fund motto

My mind will not be wasted because I intend to use it to ...

_____

_____

_____

_____

_____

_____

_____

_____

_____

_____

_____

_____

_____

_____

_____

_____

_____

_____

Today in 1944, the United Negro College Fund was founded by
Mary McLeod Bethune and F.D. Patterson to provide Black students
scholarships to attend one of thirty-seven private HBCUs.

I'm curious! Name five private HBCUs.

April 26

"If you don't like my ocean don't fish in my sea. Stay out of my valley and let my mountain be." ~ Ma Rainey

I am wonderfully made and I like me for me! A few of the things I like about myself are ...

_____

_____

_____

_____

_____

_____

_____

_____

_____

_____

_____

_____

_____

_____

_____

_____

_____

_____

Today in 1886, blues singer Gertrude "Ma" Rainey was born. She was one of the first blues singers to record her songs and is often called the "Mother of the Blues." She recorded over one hundred songs.

I'm curious! Name two musicians with whom she recorded.

April 27

"We are starting a new era of hope, reconciliation, and nation building."~ Nelson Mandela

I am starting a new era of hope. I am hoping for ...

_____

_____

_____

_____

_____

_____

_____

_____

_____

_____

_____

_____

_____

_____

_____

_____

_____

_____

Today in 1994, South Africa had its first post-apartheid elections in which Black South Africans and anyone over 18 from any race were allowed to vote. Nelson Mandela was elected as president.

I'm curious! What is the holiday on April 27th called in South Africa?

April 28

"I am going in as an American citizen, entitled to my rights, no more, no less, and I shall insist on them." ~ Attorney Arthur Mitchell

I insist on my rights! I have a right to ...

_____

_____

_____

_____

_____

_____

_____

_____

_____

_____

_____

_____

_____

_____

_____

_____

_____

Today in 1941, the Supreme Court ruled that separate but equal train laws did not apply to interstate travel. The case was presented by Arthur Mitchell, who was forcibly moved to a segregated car.

I'm curious! What was Mr. Mitchell the first to do?

April 29

"Whenever my environment had failed to support or nourish me, I had clutched at books ...." ~ Richard Wright

Reading nourishes me! My favorite book taught me ...

_____

_____

_____

_____

_____

_____

_____

_____

_____

_____

_____

_____

_____

_____

_____

_____

_____

_____

Today in 1945, Richard Wright's Black Boy reached first place on the National Best Seller Book List. In 1940, his book Native Son was selected as the first Book of the Month Club novel written by an African American.

I'm curious! What were these stories about?

April 30

"Julian Abele was the Black architect who designed Duke University thirty-seven years before he could have attended it." ~ Rachel Doyle

My contributions will last the test of time. I am contributing ...

_____

_____

_____

_____

_____

_____

_____

_____

_____

_____

_____

_____

_____

_____

_____

_____

_____

_____

_____

Today in 1881, architect Julian Abele was born. He studied in Paris, France for three years and helped design over four hundred buildings including Philadelphia's Free Library and Museum of Art.

I'm curious! What colleges have buildings designed by him?

May 1

"Salvation for a race, nation or class must come from within."
~ A. Philip Randolph

Salvation is within me. This means that...

_____

_____

_____

_____

_____

_____

_____

_____

_____

_____

_____

_____

_____

_____

_____

_____

_____

_____

Today in 1941, A. Philip Randolph issued a call for one hundred thousand Blacks to march on Washington, D.C. to protest employment discrimination in the armed forces and war industry.

I'm curious! Why did he later call off the march?

May 2

"Others tried to imitate McCoy's invention, but he kept ahead of them with his superior engineering skills." ~ Burton Folsom

I stay ahead of my imitators because my greatest competition is myself. By this I mean that...

_____

_____

_____

_____

_____

_____

_____

_____

_____

_____

_____

_____

_____

_____

_____

_____

_____

Today in 1844, inventor and engineer Elijah McCoy was born to formerly enslaved parents in Canada. He is best known for creating a train engine lubrication system for which he received a patent in 1872.

I'm curious! What do people mean by "The Real McCoy?"

May 3

"There is a method of exclusion more terrible than merely a formal one ... the gentleman alluded to (Allen) would starve in that profession"
~ Abolitionist Henry Bodwich

With courage I will press through adversity and I will ...

_____

_____

_____

_____

_____

_____

_____

_____

_____

_____

_____

_____

_____

_____

_____

_____

_____

_____

Today in 1845, Macon B. Allen passed the Massachusetts bar exam.
Allen is both the first African American licensed to practice law and
the first to hold a judicial position in the U.S.

I'm curious! How did he get to the testing site?

May 4

"If you see something that is not right, not fair, not just, you have a moral obligation to do something about it." ~ Congressman John Lewis

I will make life better by doing something about ...

_____

_____

_____

_____

_____

_____

_____

_____

_____

_____

_____

_____

_____

_____

_____

_____

_____

_____

_____

Today in 1961, thirteen Freedom Riders began bus trips through the South to test desegregation laws. Seven Blacks and six whites, including John Lewis, left the District of Columbia on a Greyhound bus headed toward New Orleans.

I'm curious! Approximately how many Freedom Rides took place?

May 5

"If I had the privilege of selecting.... I would select the race in which I was born .... for this race needs me" ~ A.C. Powell Sr.

I exist for a reason. My race needs me to ...

_____

_____

_____

_____

_____

_____

_____

_____

_____

_____

_____

_____

_____

_____

_____

_____

_____

_____

Today in 1865, community activist Adam Clayton Powell Sr. was born. He grew the Abyssinian Baptist Church in Harlem into the largest Protestant congregation in the country with thirteen thousand members.

I'm curious! What national organization did he found?

May 6

"This visionary, although long gone, is someone who has irreversibly influenced all of our lives" ~ Unknown

I have great influence because ...

_____

_____

_____

_____

_____

_____

_____

_____

_____

_____

_____

_____

_____

_____

_____

_____

_____

_____

Today in 1888, Matthew Cherry received a patent for the tricycle. He also invented the streetcar fender, metal attached to the front of streetcars. It is now used on almost every vehicle.

I'm curious! What was the purpose of the fender?

"Joe Winters: A man for all seasons." ~ Mike Marotte

I am helpful in many ways. Some of those ways include ...

_____

_____

_____

_____

_____

_____

_____

_____

_____

_____

_____

_____

_____

_____

_____

_____

_____

_____

Today in 1878, Joseph Winters received a patent for the fire escape ladders that were mounted on fire engine wagons. He later received a patent for the fire escape which are now attached to buildings.

I'm curious! In what other type of escape did he participate?

May 8
A life is not important except in the impact it has on other lives."
~ Jackie Robinson

I have positive impacts on others. I can continue doing so by ...

_____

_____

_____

_____

_____

_____

_____

_____

_____

_____

_____

_____

_____

_____

_____

_____

_____

_____

_____

Today in 1950, activist Jackie Robinson was the first African
American to be featured on the cover of Life magazine. He was the
first African American to play baseball in the Major League.

I'm curious! What teams did he play for?

May 9

"Truth is powerful and it prevails." ~ Sojourner Truth

I walk in truth and I will prevail at...

_____
_____
_____
_____
_____
_____
_____
_____
_____
_____
_____
_____
_____
_____
_____
_____
_____
_____
_____

Today in 1867, abolitionist and women's rights activist Sojourner Truth spoke at the Equal Rights Convention in New York City. She was born into slavery in Swarterkill, New York and later escaped with her infant daughter.

I'm curious! She became the first Black woman to win what?

May 10

"I strike out boldly, as if born in a desert and looking for civilization." ~ P.B.S. Pinchback

I strike out boldly with courage and support from my elders to ...

_____

_____

_____

_____

_____

_____

_____

_____

_____

_____

_____

_____

_____

_____

_____

_____

_____

_____

Today in 1837, Union Army officer and politician Pinckney Pinchback was born. He was the first African American to become governor and served Louisiana from 1872 to 1873.

I'm curious! When was the next Black governor of Louisiana elected?

May 11

"America will always side with those whom she can direct, give orders to and have those orders obeyed."
~ the Honorable Minister Louis Farrakhan Sr.

I will side with right because my people need me to...

_____

_____

_____

_____

_____

_____

_____

_____

_____

_____

_____

_____

_____

_____

_____

_____

_____

Today in 1933, the Honorable Minister Louis Farrakhan Sr. was born in New York City. In addition to being the leader of the Nation of Islam, he also organized and led the 1995 Million Man March in Washington, D.C.

I'm curious! What musical instrument did he play well?

May 12

"I respectfully remind you sir, that we have been the most patient of
all people ..... considering the treatment accorded us"
~ Jackie Robinson

I cannot always be patient. Sometimes I must...

_____

_____

_____

_____

_____

_____

_____

_____

_____

_____

_____

_____

_____

_____

_____

_____

_____

_____

Today in 1958, the Summit Meeting of National Negro Leaders was
called to intensify the campaign against discrimination. President
Eisenhower was criticized by attendees for his speech.

I'm curious! What did he say that made many upset?

May 13

"My race needs no special defense, for the past history of them in this country proves them to be equal of people anywhere."
~ Robert Smalls

I am equal to people anywhere and I will demand equality by...

_____

_____

_____

_____

_____

_____

_____

_____

_____

_____

_____

_____

_____

_____

_____

_____

_____

_____

Today in 1862, Robert Smalls and seven crew men escaped slavery by taking a Confederate ship and sailing it from Charleston, South Carolina to pick up their families and then proceeding to the Union blockade ships.

I'm curious! What political position did he later hold?

May 14

"From what we get, we can make a living; what we give, however, makes a life." ~ Arthur Ashe

Many things go into making our lives truly happy. To make my life and the lives of those around me happy, I can give ...

_____

_____

_____

_____

_____

_____

_____

_____

_____

_____

_____

_____

_____

_____

_____

_____

_____

_____

Today in 1963, Arthur Ashe became the first African American to make the Davis Cup tennis team. He was the only Black man to ever win the singles title at Wimbledon, the U.S. and Australian Open.

I'm curious! What is the mission of the Arthur Ashe Foundation?

May 15

"When it comes to success the choice is simple. You can either stand up and be counted or lie down and be counted out!"
~ Maggie L. Walker

I will not be counted out! I will be counted for ...

_____

_____

_____

_____

_____

_____

_____

_____

_____

_____

_____

_____

_____

_____

_____

_____

_____

_____

Today in 1975, Maggie L. Walker's home in Richmond, Virginia was designated a historic landmark. She was a businesswoman and civil rights activist, and the first woman to form a bank in the U.S.

I'm curious! What other jobs did she hold?

May 16
"My legacy will continue through my children."
~ John Conyers

I am a legacy. To me, being a legacy means that my parents ...

_____

_____

_____

_____

_____

_____

_____

_____

_____

_____

_____

_____

_____

_____

_____

_____

_____

Today in 1929, politician John Conyers Jr. was born in Highland Park, Michigan. He served as a U.S. Representative for Michigan from 1965 to 2017. He was the longest serving African American congressman.

I'm curious! What group did he help found in 1971?

May 17

"My love of humanity and passion for helping others inspired me to become a physician." ~ Dr. Patricia Bath

My love and passion inspires me to ...

_____

_____

_____

_____

_____

_____

_____

_____

_____

_____

_____

_____

_____

_____

_____

_____

_____

Today in 1988, ophthalmologist Patricia Bath received a patent for an apparatus that removes cataracts with laser technology, becoming the first Black woman to receive a patent for a medical purpose.

I'm curious! What are two of her other firsts?

May 18

"The thin disguise of 'equal' accommodations for passengers in railroad coaches will not mislead anyone, nor atone for the wrong this day was done." ~ Justice John Harlan

It is important that I fight injustice. It is important because ...

_____

_____

_____

_____

_____

_____

_____

_____

_____

_____

_____

_____

_____

_____

_____

_____

_____

_____

Today in 1896, Plessy v. Ferguson was a decision of the U.S. Supreme Court that upheld racial segregation laws for public facilities. This decision was used to justify discrimination for over fifty years.

I'm curious! Which justice did Justice Harlan deeply inspire with his dissent?

May 1
"The future belongs to those who prepare for it today."
~ Malcolm X

The future belongs to me! I am preparing for the future by ...

_____

_____

_____

_____

_____

_____

_____

_____

_____

_____

_____

_____

_____

_____

_____

_____

_____

_____

Today in 1925, Malcolm X was born. He was an activist who fought for
the rights of Black people. He emphasized Pan-Africanism,
self-determination, and self-defense.

I'm curious! Who was his wife?

May 20

"They have in me struck down but the trunk of the tree, the roots are many and deep — they will shoot up again!"
~ Toussaint L'Ouverture

Because of my ancestors my roots are strong! Having strong roots means that ...

_____

_____

_____

_____

_____

_____

_____

_____

_____

_____

_____

_____

_____

_____

_____

_____

_____

_____

_____

Today in 1743, Touissant L'Ouverture was born in Haiti. He led the Haitian Revolution and set the grounds for the Black army's victory in winning Haiti as a sovereign state.

I'm curious! In which year did Haiti declare independence?

May 21

"We don't always choose moments. You know, sometimes they choose us." ~ Loretta Lynch

I will be ready for my moments! I am getting ready by ...

_____

_____

_____

_____

_____

_____

_____

_____

_____

_____

_____

_____

_____

_____

_____

_____

_____

_____

Today in 1959, Loretta Lynch was born in Greensboro, North Carolina. She was appointed by President Obama to become the 83rd Attorney General of the U.S. She earned both her BA and JD from Harvard University.

I'm curious! From which HBCU did both of her parents graduate?

May 22

"No officer in this regiment now doubts that the key to the successful prosecution of this war lies in the unlimited employment of Black troops." ~ Col. Higginson

No one can doubt me because I don't doubt myself! I know that I can ...

_____

_____

_____

_____

_____

_____

_____

_____

_____

_____

_____

_____

_____

_____

_____

_____

_____

_____

Today in 1863, the Bureau of Colored Troops was created by the U.S. War Department. Unfortunately, Black men were often not treated fairly. They received lower wages and were not allowed to serve as commissioned officers.

I'm curious! What was the monthly pay for Black soldiers in the 1860s?

May 23
"There is no Hamilton without Shuffle Along."
~ Soraya McDonald

Because of my ancestors I know that I can ...

_____

_____

_____

_____

_____

_____

_____

_____

_____

_____

_____

_____

_____

_____

_____

_____

_____

Today in 1921, Shuffle Along debuted on Broadway and was produced, written and performed entirely by African Americans. It is credited with launching the Harlem Renaissance and the careers of Josephine Baker and Paul Robeson.

I'm curious! What is the plot of Shuffle Along?

May 24

"The reason people stab behind you is because you are ahead of them." ~ Alamin Mohammed Said

With the love and support of family, ancestors and community I will not be held back from ...

_____

_____

_____

_____

_____

_____

_____

_____

_____

_____

_____

_____

_____

_____

_____

_____

_____

_____

_____

Today in 1993, Eritrea achieves independence from Ethiopia after a thirty-year civil war. Famous Eritrean Americans include Tiffany Haddish, Nipsey Hussle, and Swizz Beatz.

I'm curious! Who is Eritrean American Haben Girma?

May 25

"What success I achieved is due to the fact that I have always worked just as hard where there were ten people in the house as when there were thousands." ~ Bill "Bojangles" Robinson

I always work hard. I am working hard to achieve ...

_____

_____

_____

_____

_____

_____

_____

_____

_____

_____

_____

_____

_____

_____

_____

_____

_____

_____

Today in 1877, actor, tap dancer, and activist Bill "Bojangles" Robinson was born in Richmond, Virginia. He was the best known and most highly paid Black entertainer in the first half of the twentieth century.

I'm curious! What musical did he star in that was based on his life?

May 26

"My future starts when I wake up every morning. Every day I find something creative to do with my life." ~ Miles Davis

I should have a morning routine. My routine can include ...

_____

_____

_____

_____

_____

_____

_____

_____

_____

_____

_____

_____

_____

_____

_____

_____

_____

_____

_____

Today in 1926, jazz trumpeter, bandleader, and composer Miles Davis was born in Alton, Illinois. He has been called one of the most innovative and influential musicians of his time.

I'm curious! What were his parents' professions?

May 27

"We wanted to widen options for ourselves, and later for our children." ~ Ernest Green

My ancestors widened options for me. I must widen options for myself and for my future! I can do this by ...

_____

_____

_____

_____

_____

_____

_____

_____

_____

_____

_____

_____

_____

_____

_____

_____

_____

_____

Today in 1958, Ernest Green was the first African American to graduate from Central High School in Little Rock, Arkansas. He was a member of the Little Rock Nine, a group of Black students that desegregated the school.

I'm curious! Why were these students chosen by the NAACP?

May 28

"I wish you power that equals your intelligence and strength. I wish you success that equals your talent and determination."
~ Betty Shabazz

I come from greatness! I have power and success and with these I can ...

_____

_____

_____

_____

_____

_____

_____

_____

_____

_____

_____

_____

_____

_____

_____

_____

_____

Today in 1934, civil rights advocate and educator Dr. Betty Shabazz was born. She was the wife of civil rights leader, Malcolm X and raised their six daughters after his death.

I'm curious! What are three things named in her honor?

May 29

"The only thing that will stop you from fulfilling your dreams is you." ~ Tom Bradley

I am my only competition. I will fulfill my dreams because ...

_____

_____

_____

_____

_____

_____

_____

_____

_____

_____

_____

_____

_____

_____

_____

_____

_____

Today in 1973, former police officer and attorney Thomas Bradley became the first Black mayor of Los Angeles, California. He served for twenty years, longer than anyone in the city's history.

I'm curious! What major event did he help bring to Los Angeles in 1984?

May 30

"The truth is .... everything counts. Everything we do and say.
Everything helps or hurts; everything adds to or takes away from
someone else. ~ Countee Cullen

Everything counts, including me. I am important because ...

_____

_____

_____

_____

_____

_____

_____

_____

_____

_____

_____

_____

_____

_____

_____

_____

_____

_____

_____

Today in 1903, Harlem Renaissance poet, novelist, and playwright
Countee Cullen was born. He also taught French and Writing at a New
York junior high school throughout his career.

I'm curious! Who was his first father-in-law?

May 31

"It had restaurants and furriers and jewelry stores and hotels. The white mobs looted the homes and businesses before they set fire."
~ B.C. Franklin

My spirit cannot be destroyed! It can't be destroyed because ...

_____

_____

_____

_____

_____

_____

_____

_____

_____

_____

_____

_____

_____

_____

_____

_____

_____

_____

Today in 1921, the Tulsa race massacre began when mobs of whites attacked Black residents and businesses. The attack killed between one hundred to three hundred and destroyed more than thirty-five blocks and $32 million in property.

I'm curious! What was the alleged event that started the massacre?

June 1

"It is my ambition to do good for our people who have not had the opportunity before." ~ William V. Banks

I will do good for our people by …

_____

_____

_____

_____

_____

_____

_____

_____

_____

_____

_____

_____

_____

_____

_____

_____

_____

_____

_____

_____

Today in 1973, Detroit based WPGR becomes the first African American owned television station to be given a permit to operate. It was financed by the Black branch of the Masons.

I'm curious! Who was the station president and what was his other first?

June 2

"The greatest affliction we have to suffer is the lack of trial by jury when accused of crime. Lynching of Negroes is growing to be a Southern pastime." ~ Rev. D.A. Graham

Injustice is an affliction because ...

_____

_____

_____

_____

_____

_____

_____

_____

_____

_____

_____

_____

_____

_____

_____

_____

_____

_____

Today in 1899, The Afro-American Council declared a national day of fasting to protest lynchings and violence against Black people. From 1882 to 1968 over five thousand lynchings were documented.

I'm curious! This council was the first of what type of organization?

June 3

"Excellence of performance will transcend artificial barriers created by man." ~ Dr. Charles Drew

My excellence will transcend artificial barriers! I am excellent at ...

_____

_____

_____

_____

_____

_____

_____

_____

_____

_____

_____

_____

_____

_____

_____

_____

_____

_____

Today in 1904, Dr. Charles Drew was born in Washington, D.C. He was a surgeon and a medical researcher who developed improved techniques for blood storage and helped develop blood banks during World War II.

I'm curious! Why did he resign from the American Red Cross?

June 4

"Don't let anyone rob you of your imagination, your creativity, or your curiosity.." ~ Dr. Mae Jemison

I will not be robbed of my imagination, creativity or curiosity! I am protecting my greatness by ...

_____

_____

_____

_____

_____

_____

_____

_____

_____

_____

_____

_____

_____

_____

_____

_____

_____

Today in 1987, Dr. Mae Jemison was chosen by NASA to begin training as a space shuttle astronaut. She became the first African American woman to travel to space in 1992.

I'm curious! What was her first profession?

June 5

"Doris never gave up her belief in the people of the City of Compton." ~ Unknown

I will never give up my belief in the people because ...

_____

_____

_____

_____

_____

_____

_____

_____

_____

_____

_____

_____

_____

_____

_____

_____

_____

_____

_____

Today in 1973, Doris A. Davis became mayor of Compton, California, making her the first Black woman to govern a metropolitan city. She also founded a child development center.

I'm curious! How many years did she direct the center?

June 6

"Service is the rent we pay for being. It is the very purpose of life, and not something you do in your spare time."
~ Marian Wright Edelman

I will serve my community by ...

_____

_____

_____

_____

_____

_____

_____

_____

_____

_____

_____

_____

_____

_____

_____

_____

_____

Today in 1939, Marian Wright Edelman was born in Bennetsville, South Carolina. She became the first Black female lawyer in Mississippi and the founder and president emerita of the Children's Defense Fund.

I'm curious! Why did she get arrested in 1960?

June 7

"Despite everything, no one can dictate who you are to other people."
~ Prince

Only I can dictate who I am! I am ...

_____

_____

_____

_____

_____

_____

_____

_____

_____

_____

_____

_____

_____

_____

_____

_____

_____

_____

Today in 1958, songwriter, musician, filmmaker, and activist Prince Rogers Nelson was born in Minneapolis, Minnesota. He was one of the best-selling musicians of all times and released sixty-eight albums.

I'm curious! What was the name of his charity?

June 8

"Demonstrating her unwavering benevolence, the 1930
census lists fourteen adopted sons and daughters,
ages 11 to 19, livingin her household."
~ Virginia Women's Monument

I will demonstrate unwavering benevolence by ...

_____

_____

_____

_____

_____

_____

_____

_____

_____

_____

_____

_____

_____

_____

_____

_____

_____

Today in 1874, pioneer of vocational training, Virginia E. Randolph was
born in Richmond, Virginia. She received funding to maintain rural
Black schools in the south teaching academics, woodworking, sewing,
and more.

I'm curious! What organization did she help found a Black branch of?

June 9

"Art must be the quintessence of meaning. Creative art means that you create yourself." ~ Meta Vaux Warrick

I create myself. In myself I see...

_____

_____

_____

_____

_____

_____

_____

_____

_____

_____

_____

_____

_____

_____

_____

_____

_____

_____

Today in 1877, Harlem Renaissance sculptor and artist Meta Vaux Warrick was born in Philadelphia, Pennsylvania. She studied in Paris, France and created significant work that visualized Black culture and suffering.

I'm curious! What was her childhood like?

June 10

"Faith is the Black person's federal reserve system."
~ Hattie McDaniel

My faith is important because ...

_____

_____

_____

_____

_____

_____

_____

_____

_____

_____

_____

_____

_____

_____

_____

_____

_____

Today in 1893, actress and singer Hattie McDaniel was born to formerly enslaved parents in Wichita, Kansas. In 1940, she was the first African American to win an Academy Award.
She appeared in over three hundred films.

I'm curious! Which HBCU did she request that her Oscar be given?

June 11

"You must always be ready to seize the moment..." ~ Vivian Malone

I am ready to seize the moment because I have been preparing. I have been preparing by...

_____
_____
_____
_____
_____
_____
_____
_____
_____
_____
_____
_____
_____
_____
_____
_____
_____
_____
_____

Today in 1963, Governor George Wallace stood in the door of the auditorium of the University of Alabama to block the entry of two African Americans, Vivian Malone and James Hood, as they tried to register for classes.

I'm curious! Why did he finally move?

June 12

"I support the freedom to marry for all. That's what Loving, and loving, are all about." ~ Mildred Loving

I come from love therefore I am love. I know that I am love because...

_____

_____

_____

_____

_____

_____

_____

_____

_____

_____

_____

_____

_____

_____

_____

_____

_____

_____

Today in 1967, Loving v. Virginia found that laws banning interracial marriage violated the Fourteenth Amendment. Mildred and Richard Loving were sentenced to a year in prison in 1958 for marrying.

I'm curious! What year did Alabama adapt its laws to the Court's decision?

June 13

"Each of you must pick your own goals. Listen to others,
but do not become a blind follower." ~ Thurgood Marshall

I am a leader and not a follower! I pick my own goals. My goals are …

_____

_____

_____

_____

_____

_____

_____

_____

_____

_____

_____

_____

_____

_____

_____

_____

_____

_____

_____

Today in 1967, Thurgood Marshall, the first African American U.S.
Supreme Court justice, was nominated by President Lyndon Johnson.
He was born in Baltimore, Maryland and attended two HBCUs.

I'm curious! What cases did he argue in front of the U.S.
Supreme Court?

June 14
"We are all gifted. That is our inheritance."
~ Ethel Waters

I am gifted! A few of my gifts are...

_____

_____

_____

_____

_____

_____

_____

_____

_____

_____

_____

_____

_____

_____

_____

_____

_____

_____

Today in 1939, the Ethel Waters Show premiered on NBC as the first special starred in by a Black performer. She was also the first African American to integrate Broadway.

I'm curious! Who was the first Black person to appear on TV?

June 15
"I refused to take no for an answer." ~ Bessie Coleman

I refuse to take no for an answer! I will ...

_____

_____

_____

_____

_____

_____

_____

_____

_____

_____

_____

_____

_____

_____

_____

_____

_____

_____

Today in 1921, Bessie Coleman became the first African American woman to earn an international aviation license in Paris, France and first female African American pilot.

I'm curious! How many children did her parents have?

June 16

"Once the door opens you step across the threshold and you're in the game." ~ Adam Wade

I'm in the game and while I'm on the court I'm going to …

_____

_____

_____

_____

_____

_____

_____

_____

_____

_____

_____

_____

_____

_____

_____

_____

_____

Today in 1975, musician and actor Adam Wade became the first African American to host a television game show. He also released thirty-five songs and appeared in Black sitcoms and blaxploitation movies.

I'm curious! What was the name of his game show?

June 17

"Shadowed beneath Thy hand /May we forever stand/True to our God/True to our native land." ~ James W. Johnson

True to my God, true to my native land may I forever stand for …

_____

_____

_____

_____

_____

_____

_____

_____

_____

_____

_____

_____

_____

_____

_____

_____

_____

_____

Today 1871, educator, author, activist, and lawyer James Weldon Johnson was born. He was a leader in the Harlem Renaissance and served as the first secretary of the NAACP.

I'm curious! What song did he write in 1900?

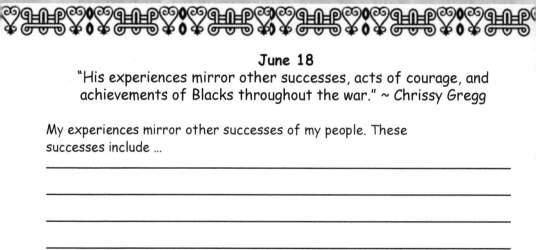

June 18

"His experiences mirror other successes, acts of courage, and achievements of Blacks throughout the war." ~ Chrissy Gregg

My experiences mirror other successes of my people. These successes include …

_____

_____

_____

_____

_____

_____

_____

_____

_____

_____

_____

_____

_____

_____

_____

_____

_____

_____

Today in 1942, Dr. Bernard W. Robinson became the first Black Naval officer. He attended Harvard Medical School and served in the Veterans Hospital System for the rest of his career.

I'm curious! What kind of medical doctor was he?

June 19

"The people of Texas are informed that in accordance with a Proclamation ..., all slaves are free." ~ Gen. Granger

I am free! I am free to be who the Creator made me to be. Being free means that ...

_____

_____

_____

_____

_____

_____

_____

_____

_____

_____

_____

_____

_____

_____

_____

_____

_____

Today in 1865, the emancipation announcement was made in Galveston, Texas signaling that the last remaining enslaved people in the U.S. were free.

I'm curious! What holiday commemorates this day?

June 20

"I always like to challenge myself. I never want to be put into a box."
~ Lionel Richie

I have a purpose and can't be put into a box! Today, I challenge myself to …

_____

_____

_____

_____

_____

_____

_____

_____

_____

_____

_____

_____

_____

_____

_____

_____

_____

_____

_____

Today in 1949, singer-songwriter Lionel Richie was born in Tuskegee, Alabama. He graduated from Tuskegee University with a degree in Economics. He has sold over ninety million records.

I'm curious! What R&B group was he a member of?

June 21

"We must believe in the ability of man to respond to the problems of his environment." ~ Carl B. Stokes

I will respond to the problems in my environment by ...

_____

_____

_____

_____

_____

_____

_____

_____

_____

_____

_____

_____

_____

_____

_____

_____

_____

_____

_____

Today in 1927, attorney, politician, and municipal judge Carl B. Stokes was born in Cleveland, Ohio. Taking office in 1968, he was the first Black elected mayor of a major U.S. city.

I'm curious! What other first did he achieve in 1972?

June 22

"People in your life are important. Meaningful relationships with those people are very important." ~ Ed Bradley

Meaningful relationships are very important because ...

_____
_____
_____
_____
_____
_____
_____
_____
_____
_____
_____
_____
_____
_____
_____
_____
_____
_____

Today in 1941, journalist Ed Bradley was born in Philadelphia, Pennsylvania. He graduated from Cheyney State University and did over five hundred stories during his twenty-six years on CBS' 60 Minutes.

I'm curious! What political first did he achieve?

June 23

"I believe in me more than anything in this world." ~ Wilma Rudolph

My elders believe in me. My family believes in me. I believe in me and I know that I can ...

_____

_____

_____

_____

_____

_____

_____

_____

_____

_____

_____

_____

_____

_____

_____

_____

_____

_____

_____

Today in 1940, track and field star Wilma Rudolph was born. She won a Bronze Olympic medal in 1956 and became the first American woman to win three gold medals in a single game in 1960.

I'm curious! From which HBCU did she graduate after the Olympics?

June 24
"I came here with the campaign to tell people that we got to be treated like human beings" ~ Henrietta Franklin

My ancestors fought for me to be treated like a human being and I won't forget it because ...

_____

_____

_____

_____

_____

_____

_____

_____

_____

_____

_____

_____

_____

_____

_____

_____

_____

_____

Today in 1968, Resurrection City in Washington, D.C was closed after six weeks and two hundred and eighty-eight people were arrested. It was an extended occupation of the Poor People's Campaign on the National Mall by three thousand demonstrators.

I'm curious! What was the purpose of the campaign?

June 25

"When it comes to my rights as an American citizen, and yours, I am a triumphalist and an absolutist. Anything less is an insult."
~ James Meredith

For our rights I am a triumphalist and an absolutist! This means that I ...

_____

_____

_____

_____

_____

_____

_____

_____

_____

_____

_____

_____

_____

_____

_____

_____

_____

_____

Today in 1933, Civil Rights activist James Meredith was born. He became the first African American student admitted to the University of Mississippi. He advocated for voter registration.

I'm curious! What ended his March Against Fear on the second day?

June 26

"The only places on earth not to provide free public education are China, N. Vietnam, Sarawak, Singapore, and Prince Edward County, VA"
~ Robert F. Kennedy

I have the ability to fulfill my purpose! I will not take my education for granted and instead I will ...

_____

_____

_____

_____

_____

_____

_____

_____

_____

_____

_____

_____

_____

_____

_____

_____

_____

Today in 1959, officials in Prince Edward County, Virginia voted to close their public schools rather than integrate which was required by law. The schools remained closed for the next five years.

I'm curious! How did this impact Black teachers and students?

June 27

"We wear the mask that grins and lies."
~ Paul Laurence Dunbar

I will not wear any mask that hides my greatness because ...

_____
_____
_____
_____
_____
_____
_____
_____
_____
_____
_____
_____
_____
_____
_____
_____
_____
_____

Today in 1872, novelist and poet Paul Laurence Dunbar was born in Dayton, Ohio to formerly enslaved parents. He became one of the first Black writers to become known internationally.

I'm curious! For which all Black musical did he write the lyrics?

June 28

"We want freedom, justice, and equality by any means necessary.
We want it now ...." ~ Malcolm X

When Malcolm X said by any means necessary he meant ...

_____

_____

_____

_____

_____

_____

_____

_____

_____

_____

_____

_____

_____

_____

_____

_____

_____

_____

Today in 1964, Malcolm X founded the Organization of Afro-American Unity. One of the purposes of the organization was to fight for the human rights of African Americans.

I'm curious! What were the other purposes of the OAAU?

June 29

"Our grandfathers had to run, run, run. My generation's out of breath.
We ain't running no more." ~ Stokely Carmichael

I don't have to run so I am not running! I am not running from ...

_____

_____

_____

_____

_____

_____

_____

_____

_____

_____

_____

_____

_____

_____

_____

_____

_____

_____

_____

Today in 1941, Freedom Rider and civil rights activist Stokely
Carmichael was born in Trinidad. He graduated from Howard
University and developed the Black Power Movement.

I'm curious! What position did he hold with the Black Panthers?

June 30

"You have to be taught to be second class; you're not born that way." ~ Lena Horne

I was born first class! This means that I can ...

_____

_____

_____

_____

_____

_____

_____

_____

_____

_____

_____

_____

_____

_____

_____

_____

_____

Today 1917, entertainer and activist Lena Horne was born in Brooklyn, New York. Her career spanned over seventy years and she appear in film, theater, and TV. She was deeply committed to the Civil Rights Movement.

I'm curious! Where did she refuse to perform?

July 1

"If you don't like something, change it. If you can't change it, change your attitude." ~ Michelle Howard

I can change it! Having the power of change means that I can...

_____

_____

_____

_____

_____

_____

_____

_____

_____

_____

_____

_____

_____

_____

_____

_____

_____

_____

Today in 2014, Michelle Howard was the first woman to become a four-star admiral in the U.S. Navy. She also made history in 1999 as the first African American woman to captain a U.S. naval ship.

I'm curious! What is one of her other historic firsts?

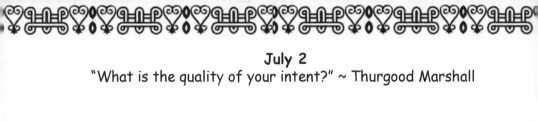

July 2
"What is the quality of your intent?" ~ Thurgood Marshall

My intent is of great quality! To me, this means that …

_____

_____

_____

_____

_____

_____

_____

_____

_____

_____

_____

_____

_____

_____

_____

_____

_____

_____

Today in 1908, the first African American U.S. Supreme Court Judge Thurgood Marshall was born. He was born in Baltimore, Maryland and graduated from Lincoln University and Howard University School of Law.

I'm curious! How did he help schools in the U.S.?

July 3

"The passion of fear, like pride and envy, hath slain its
thousands." ~ Prince Hall

When I need help I can call on my ancestors, my community and my family. I
will not be afraid to ...

_____

_____

_____

_____

_____

_____

_____

_____

_____

_____

_____

_____

_____

_____

_____

_____

_____

_____

Today in 1775, Prince Hall founded African Lodge No. 1, the first
Black lodge of Free Masons in the U.S. Prince Hall was an abolitionist
who fought for education rights for Black children.

I'm curious! In what movement was he active?

July 4

"No race can prosper till it learns that there is as much dignity in tilling a field as in writing a poem." ~ Booker T. Washington

Everyday I take great dignity in writing in my journal. I write in this journal because it helps me to...

_____

_____

_____

_____

_____

_____

_____

_____

_____

_____

_____

_____

_____

_____

_____

_____

_____

_____

Today in 1881, Tuskegee Institute was established by Booker T. Washington. It was home to World War II's Tuskegee Airmen and scientist George Washington Carver. The University graduates more than seventy percent of Black veterinarians.

I'm curious! Who are two famous Tuskegee alumnae?

July 5
"Start where you are. Use what you have. Do what you can."
~ Arthur Ashe

I will do what I can for myself, my family and my community! I can...

_____

_____

_____

_____

_____

_____

_____

_____

_____

_____

_____

_____

_____

_____

_____

_____

_____

_____

Today in 1975, tennis player Arthur Ashe became the first African American male to win a singles title at Wimbledon. Prior to this, he was awarded a tennis scholarship to UCLA.

I'm curious! What did he achieve as a Lieutenant in the Army?

July 6

"From far back, I was interested in discovering new things and knowing exactly how objects worked." ~ Henry T. Sampson

Curiosity is powerful and can lead to greater understanding. I am curious about ...

_____

_____

_____

_____

_____

_____

_____

_____

_____

_____

_____

_____

_____

_____

_____

_____

_____

_____

Today in 1971, Henry Sampson was awarded a patent for technology that is used in today's cell phones. He attended Morehouse and later became the first Black person to earn a PhD in Nuclear Engineering.

I'm curious! What was the subject of his authored books?

July 7

"Work like you don't need the money. Love like you've never been hurt.
Dance like nobody's watching." ~ Satchel Paige

I am love and I am worth being happy! I will dance like nobody's watching
because …

_____

_____

_____

_____

_____

_____

_____

_____

_____

_____

_____

_____

_____

_____

_____

_____

_____

_____

Today in 1906, baseball player Satchel Paige was born in Mobile, Alabama.
He played for the Negro and Major Baseball Leagues. His professional
career lasted from 1926-1966 and he attracted record crowds.

I'm curious! What are some of the teams that he played for?

July 8

"Geniuses have a little extra something. There's that little something that you know is a little different." ~ Billy Eckstine

I am a genius and a little different and that is more than okay! I am unique because ...

_____

_____

_____

_____

_____

_____

_____

_____

_____

_____

_____

_____

_____

_____

_____

_____

_____

_____

Today in 1914, jazz singer Billy Eckstine was born in Pittsburgh, Pennsylvania. He worked with many jazz greats including Dizzy Gillespie, Miles Davis, and Sarah Vaughan.

I'm curious! How long did his career span?

July 9

"But I stayed the course, because no soldier should desert his post because he may be overcome." ~ E. Frederic Morrow

I am loyal to those who need me. I will stay the course because ...

_____

_____

_____

_____

_____

_____

_____

_____

_____

_____

_____

_____

_____

_____

_____

_____

_____

_____

Today in 1955, E. Frederic Morrow was appointed administrative aide to President Eisenhower, making him the first African American to hold an executive position in the White House.

I'm curious! In 1964, what job did he begin?

July 10

"If we have the courage of our forbearers, ... we shall find a way to do for our day what they did for theirs." ~ Mary McLeod Bethune

I have the courage of our forbearers! I will find a way to ...

_____

_____

_____

_____

_____

_____

_____

_____

_____

_____

_____

_____

_____

_____

_____

_____

_____

Today in 1875, Mary McLeod Bethune is born in Mayesville, South Carolina. She founded Bethune-Cookman University and co-founded the United Negro College Fund. She also founded the National Council of Negro Women.

I'm curious! What Black organization was first to be headquartered in D.C.?

July 11

"A true and worthy ideal frees and uplifts a people; a false ideal imprisons and lowers." ~ W.E.B. Du Bois

I will contribute true and worthy ideals! A few of my ideals include ...

_____

_____

_____

_____

_____

_____

_____

_____

_____

_____

_____

_____

_____

_____

_____

_____

_____

_____

_____

Today in 1905, W.E.B. Du Bois and delegates from fourteen states organized the Niagara Movement to demand abolition of all distinctions based on race. It was a forerunner to the NAACP.

I'm curious! Why was this name chosen?

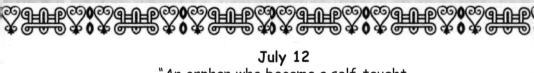

July 12

"An orphan who became a self-taught
mechanical wizard, scientist, and developer."
~ Frederick Jones' eulogist

I can rise from trials to triumph! I will rise and I will be triumphant in my
goals of ..._____

_____

_____

_____

_____

_____

_____

_____

_____

_____

_____

_____

_____

_____

_____

_____

_____

_____

Today in 1949, inventor Frederick Jones received a patent for an
automatic refrigeration system for long-haul trucks. He was awarded
sixty-one patents for sound equipment, x-ray machines, and
gas engines.

I'm curious! He was the first African American to win what in 1991?

July 13

"The New York City Draft Riot remains the bloodiest outbreak of civil disorder in American history." ~ M. Kentake

My ancestors are counting on me to make a change. One thing I want to change is...

_____

_____

_____

_____

_____

_____

_____

_____

_____

_____

_____

_____

_____

_____

_____

_____

_____

_____

Today in 1863, the New York City draft riots began when whites were angered by laws passed to draft men into the war. Afraid that they would take their jobs, white people attacked Black people killing one hundred and nineteen and injuring two thousand.

I'm curious! How many white people were convicted for this violence?

July 14
In order to free ourselves we must be ourselves."
~ Maulana Karenga

I will be my true myself! I describe myself as...

_____

_____

_____

_____

_____

_____

_____

_____

_____

_____

_____

_____

_____

_____

_____

_____

_____

_____

Today in 1941, activist Maulana Karenga was born in Maryland. He
created Kwanzaa in 1966 to give African Americans an opportunity to
celebrate themselves and their history.

I'm curious! What are the seven principles of Kwanzaa?

July 15
"Education and work are the levers to uplift a people."
~ W.E.B. Du Bois

I am uplifted! Being uplifted means that I am...

_____

_____

_____

_____

_____

_____

_____

_____

_____

_____

_____

_____

_____

_____

_____

_____

_____

_____

_____

Today in 1822, Philadelphia became one of the first major cities to
open public schools to African Americans. The first school was for
boys. It wasn't until 1826 that a school for girls was open.

I'm curious! When did schools in Philadelphia desegregate?

July 16

"The way to right wrongs is to turn the light of truth upon them." ~ Ida B.

Wells With the light of truth lighting my path I will right wrongs! Some wrongs I want to right include ...

_____

_____

_____

_____

_____

_____

_____

_____

_____

_____

_____

_____

_____

_____

_____

_____

_____

_____

Today in 1862, journalist, educator, and activist Ida B. Wells was born into slavery. She often wrote about segregation, inequality, and lynchings to bring attention to the plight of African Americans.

I'm curious! What HBCUs did she attend?

July 17

"If you're not invited to the party, throw your own."
~ Diahann Carroll

I will throw my own party and not compromise my integrity to have others
accept me. At my party there will be...

_____

_____

_____

_____

_____

_____

_____

_____

_____

_____

_____

_____

_____

_____

_____

_____

_____

_____

_____

Today in 1935, Diahann Carrol was born in the Bronx, New York. She was
the first Black woman to star in a non-stereotypical role on television
and to win a Tony Award for best actress in a Broadway musical.

I'm curious! What was the name of her 1968 television series?

July 18
"A winner is a dreamer who never gives up."
~ Nelson Mandela

I was born a winner! I won't give up and will keep trying to...

_____

_____

_____

_____

_____

_____

_____

_____

_____

_____

_____

_____

_____

_____

_____

_____

_____

Today in 1918, Nelson Mandela was born in South Africa. He was an anti-apartheid revolutionary, political prisoner, and the first president elected in a democratic election.

I'm curious! How long was he imprisoned?

July 19

"If my life has any meaning at all, it is that those who start out as outcasts can wind up as being part of the system."
~ P.R. Harris

My life was ordained with meaning and a purpose! Part of my purpose is…

_____

_____

_____

_____

_____

_____

_____

_____

_____

_____

_____

_____

_____

_____

_____

_____

_____

_____

Today in 1979, Patricia R. Harris was named Secretary of Health and Human Services. She was the first Black woman to serve in the cabinet and the first to represent the U.S. as an ambassador.

I'm curious! Which agency did she previously serve as secretary?

July 20

"Take it slow we've got a long way to go but we have each other and the world." ~ Ron Karenga to Amiri Baraka

We have each other and the world. It is important to have a support system because...

_____

_____

_____

_____

_____

_____

_____

_____

_____

_____

_____

_____

_____

_____

_____

_____

_____

Today in 1967, the first Black Power Conference was held in Newark, New Jersey with over one thousand people. The Manifesto was adopted and called for a "philosophy of Blackness" to promote unity.

I'm curious! What did The Manifesto condemn?

July 21

"And so, lifting as we climb, onward & upward we go, struggling & striving, & hoping ....." ~ Mary Church Terrell

I will lift as I climb. I am striving and hoping for...

_____

_____

_____

_____

_____

_____

_____

_____

_____

_____

_____

_____

_____

_____

_____

_____

_____

_____

Today in 1896, the National Association of Colored Women (NACW) was formed. Mary Church Terrell was elected president at their first meeting at Nineteenth Street Baptist Church in Washington, D.C.

I'm curious! What is the mission of NACW?

July 22

"I wasn't concerned about first, second, or last. My work was my primary concern." ~ Jane Bolin

My work is part of my purpose. My work is my concern and with my work I will ...

_____

_____

_____

_____

_____

_____

_____

_____

_____

_____

_____

_____

_____

_____

_____

_____

_____

_____

_____

Today in 1939, Jane Bolin became the first Black woman to serve as a judge when she was appointed to the Domestic Relations Court. She was also the first Black woman to graduate from Yale University Law School.

I'm curious! How long did she serve New York as a judge?

July 23

"God put flowers of many sorts and many colors on earth. The beauty of each enhancing that of the others." ~W.G. Still

I am capable of enhancing others. The positive enhancement that I bring is my ability to...

_____

_____

_____

_____

_____

_____

_____

_____

_____

_____

_____

_____

_____

_____

_____

_____

_____

_____

Today in 1936, William Grant Still became the first African American to conduct a major American orchestra, conducting the Los Angeles Philharmonic. He was educated at Wilberforce University.

I'm curious! What other first did he experience in 1949?

July 24

I risk my all upon thy power to free my brethren, fetter'd slaves, from sinking in inglorious graves. ~ Ira Aldridge

My ancestors risked it all for me so that I could achieve the dreams they couldn't. Because of them, I can...

_____

_____

_____

_____

_____

_____

_____

_____

_____

_____

_____

_____

_____

_____

_____

_____

_____

Today in 1807, Shakespearian actor and playwright Ira Aldridge was born in New York, New York. He is the only Black actor honored with a bronze plaque at the Shakespeare Memorial Theater.

I'm curious! What HBCU's theater is named in his honor?

July 25

"When troubles rise, children must be anchored so deeply that, though they sway, they will not topple." ~ Mamie Till

Because I am deeply anchored in love, strength and traditions I know that I can...

_____

_____

_____

_____

_____

_____

_____

_____

_____

_____

_____

_____

_____

_____

_____

_____

_____

_____

_____

Today in 1941, Emmett Till was born in Chicago. He was lynched in Money, Mississippi in 1955 after a white women lied, saying that he whistled at her. Following his murder, he became an icon of the Civil Rights Movement.

I'm curious! What did his mother do to show the brutal nature of hate?

July 26

"There must be no dual standards of justice, no duel rights,
privileges, duties... No dual forms of freedom." ~ A.P. Randolph

I want complete freedom! Having complete freedom means...

_____

_____

_____

_____

_____

_____

_____

_____

_____

_____

_____

_____

_____

_____

_____

_____

_____

_____

Today in 1948, President Truman issued an executive order demanding
equal treatment and opportunity in the armed forces. It was
intended to abolish discrimination based on color and race.

I'm curious! This led to the end of segregation during which war?

July 27
"The love of liberty brought us here."
~ Liberian National Motto

I am liberated! Being liberated means that...

_____

_____

_____

_____

_____

_____

_____

_____

_____

_____

_____

_____

_____

_____

_____

_____

_____

_____

Today in 1847, the first republic set up by formerly enslaved people
was established. They departed the port in New York City in 1820 and
landed in Sierra Leone. They later moved to present day Monrovia.

I'm curious! In what country is Monrovia located?

July 28

"I said 'Thank you, Lord'—not because I was alive, because I had done what I should do, and I'd done it well." ~ C.T. Vivian

I will do what I should do and do it well. A few things that I should do well are...

_____

_____

_____

_____

_____

_____

_____

_____

_____

_____

_____

_____

_____

_____

_____

_____

_____

_____

Today in 1924, minister and civil rights activist, C.T. Vivian was born. He helped organize sit-ins, marches, and freedom rides, and was the first of Martin Luther King Jr.'s staff to write a civil rights book.

I'm curious! What education program did he found and direct?

July 29
"The plain and simple gospel suits best for any people."
~ Bishop Richard Allen

I can be simple, I can be complex. To me this means that I...

_____

_____

_____

_____

_____

_____

_____

_____

_____

_____

_____

_____

_____

_____

_____

_____

_____

_____

Today in 1794, Mother Bethel AME was dedicated. It is the oldest AME congregation in the nation and the oldest church property in the U.S. to be continuously owned by African Americans.

I'm curious! In what city is Mother Bethel located?

July 30

"I did what my conscience told me to do, and you can't fail if you do that." ~ Anita Hill

I will listen to my conscience! My conscience tells me that...

_____
_____
_____
_____
_____
_____
_____
_____
_____
_____
_____
_____
_____
_____
_____
_____
_____
_____

Today in 1956, lawyer and women's rights advocate, Anita Hill was born in Lone Tree, Oklahoma. She testified against nominee Clarence Thomas' appointment to the U.S. Supreme Court in 1991.

I'm curious! What has she done since the 1991 hearing?

July 31

"Today, five years ago I entered this college. What a change. Then, I was nothing, now I am a Catholic." ~ Rev. Patrick Healy

I am somebody! I am...

_____

_____

_____

_____

_____

_____

_____

_____

_____

_____

_____

_____

_____

_____

_____

_____

_____

_____

_____

Today in 1874, Rev. Patrick Francis Healy was appointed as president of Georgetown University, the first Black president of any predominately white institution. He was born into slavery in Macon, Georgia in 1834.

I'm curious! What were his other firsts?

August 1

"In 1937 Jackie Ormes created and took charge of how she wanted a woman of color to be represented" ~ Susan Reib

I will take charge of how I am represented! I want to be represented

_____

_____

_____

_____

_____

_____

_____

_____

_____

_____

_____

_____

_____

_____

_____

_____

_____

_____

Today in 1911, artist Jackie Ormes, the first Black female cartoonist, was born in Pittsburgh, Pennsylvania. In 1947, she produced Patty-Jo, the first Black doll to have a realistic face and an upscale wardrobe.

I'm curious! What was the name of her most famous character?

August 2

"I can't believe what you say, because I see what you do."
~ James Baldwin

It is not enough to say the right thing; it is also important to do the right thing. I will make sure that my actions match my words because...

_____

_____

_____

_____

_____

_____

_____

_____

_____

_____

_____

_____

_____

_____

_____

_____

Today in 1924, James Baldwin was born. He wrote The Fire NextTime and Remember This House which became the basis of the documentary I Am Not Your Negro.

I'm curious! How old was he when he wrote "Harlem— Then and Now."

August 3

"Create sentiment favorable to intellectual and industrial liberty."
~ Lt. Colonel Allen Allensworth

I will be mindful of the feelings I create! This means that I...

_____

_____

_____

_____

_____

_____

_____

_____

_____

_____

_____

_____

_____

_____

_____

_____

_____

_____

Today in 1908, Lt. Colonel Allen Allensworth filed site plan for the first Black town, Allensworth. The town was created so that we could govern, finance and live free of racial discrimination.

I'm curious! What state was Allensworth in?

August 4

"Don't settle for what you already know. Never stop believing in the power of your ideas, your imagination, your hard work to change the world." ~ President Barack Obama

I will not stop believing in my power! I have the power to...

_____

_____

_____

_____

_____

_____

_____

_____

_____

_____

_____

_____

_____

_____

_____

_____

_____

_____

_____

Today in 1961, President Obama was born in Honolulu, Hawaii. He served as the forty-fourth president and was the 2009 Nobel Peace Prize laureate. He has been placed in the upper tier of presidents by historians.

I'm curious! Where was President Obama's father born?

August 5
"If you can be the best, then why not try to be the best?"
~ Garrett Morgan

I can, so I will! I will try to be the best by...

_____

_____

_____

_____

_____

_____

_____

_____

_____

_____

_____

_____

_____

_____

_____

_____

_____

Today in 1914, the first traffic electric lights, invented by Garrett Morgan, are installed in Cleveland, Ohio. He also invented the smoke hood, a sewing machine, and a hair straightener.

I'm curious! How did he use the smoke hood in 1916?

August 6

"There is no such thing as a vote that doesn't matter. It all matters." ~ President Barack Obama

I will exercise my right to vote! It is important that I exercise my right to vote because...

_____

_____

_____

_____

_____

_____

_____

_____

_____

_____

_____

_____

_____

_____

_____

_____

_____

_____

_____

Today in 1965, President Johnson signed the Voting Rights Act, outlawing the literacy test for voting eligibility. Poll taxes and property-ownership requirements were also banned.

I'm curious! What other tests were used to restrict voting rights?

August 7

"After the ushers said, 'No, you can't come in,' we said, 'Well, would you let Jesus in?' They said, 'This is our church, what does He have to do with it?'" ~ Rev. Ed King

I will never let hate distract me from my purpose! My purpose is bigger than me because my purpose...

_____

_____

_____

_____

_____

_____

_____

_____

_____

_____

_____

_____

_____

_____

_____

_____

Today in 1960, twenty-five students from PWIs and HBCUs started a "kneel-in" campaign that exposed the hypocrisy that existed in white churches that would not allow Blacks to enter. Protests continued throughout the 1960s

I'm curious! What is hypocrisy?

August 8

"A great person always stands taller than his tombstone"
~ Rev. Cecil Murray

I will remember the greatness of my ancestors. A few things about my ancestors that I should remember are...

_____

_____

_____

_____

_____

_____

_____

_____

_____

_____

_____

_____

_____

_____

_____

_____

_____

_____

Today in 1934, Julian Dixon was born in Washington, D.C. He served as a congressman from 1978 until his death in 2000. He chaired the Congressional Black Caucus and the House Ethics Committee.

I'm curious! What are three things named in his honor?

August 9

"I decided long ago never to walk in anyone's shadow; if I fail,
or if I succeed at least I did as I believe." ~ Linda Creed

I will stand proudly as myself! I will not walk in anyone's shadow because...

_____

_____

_____

_____

_____

_____

_____

_____

_____

_____

_____

_____

_____

_____

_____

_____

_____

_____

Today in 1963, singer and actress Whitney Houston was born. She
is one of the bestselling and most awarded female artists of all time
with two hundred million records sold worldwide.

I'm curious! What three movies did she star in?

August 10
"Peace produced by suppression is neither natural nor desirable."
~ Dr. Anna Julia Cooper

I will not be suppressed! A few things I can do to make sure that I am not suppressed are...

_____

_____

_____

_____

_____

_____

_____

_____

_____

_____

_____

_____

_____

_____

_____

_____

_____

Today in 1858, activist Dr. Anna J. Cooper was born enslaved in Raleigh, North Carolina. She became the fourth Black woman to earn a doctoral degree and is called "the Mother of Black Feminism."

I'm curious! What was the name of her first book?

August 11

"In every conceivable manner, the family is link to our past, bridge to our future." ~ Alex Haley

Family is important because...

_____

_____

_____

_____

_____

_____

_____

_____

_____

_____

_____

_____

_____

_____

_____

_____

_____

_____

_____

Today in 1921, Alex Haley was born in Ithaca, New York. He wrote the book Roots in 1976, which was adapted into a television miniseries. He also wrote The Autobiography of Malcom X.

I'm curious! What blaxploitation screenplay did he write?

August 12

"Who are the happiest people? The people who think the most interesting thoughts. Enjoying the arts gives the inner-soul nourishment essential to healthy thinking." ~ Lillian Evanti

I think interesting thoughts. Some of the things I think about are...

_____

_____

_____

_____

_____

_____

_____

_____

_____

_____

_____

_____

_____

_____

_____

_____

_____

_____

Today in 1890, opera singer Lillian Evanti was born in D.C. She traveled across Europe and South America and became the first African American to sing with an organized European company.

I'm curious! From which HBCU did she graduate?

August 13

"You can't educate a child who isn't healthy, and you can't keep a child healthy who isn't educated." ~ Dr. Joycelyn Elders

I will be healthy in body and my mind, educated about my history and purposeful about my future. This means that...

_____

_____

_____

_____

_____

_____

_____

_____

_____

_____

_____

_____

_____

_____

_____

_____

_____

_____

Today in 1933, Dr. Joycelyn Elders was born in Schaal, Arkansas. She was appointed as the first African American Surgeon General of the U.S. in 1993. She is an alumnus of Philander Smith College.

I'm curious! What job was she appointed to in 1987?

August 14

"A group is often slower to see the flame of truth than a single open-minded individual." ~ Dr. Ernest Just

I will always seek the truth and be open-minded. To be open-minded means...

_____

_____

_____

_____

_____

_____

_____

_____

_____

_____

_____

_____

_____

_____

_____

_____

_____

_____

Today in 1883, biologist Dr. Ernest Just was born in Charleston, South Carolina. He graduated from Dartmouth College and won several awards and honors and later established Omega Psi Phi fraternity in 1911.

I'm curious! What are the names of the two books he authored?

August 15
"Everyone has a part to play. We have the power. You can do it."
~ Maxine Waters

I have a part to play. I have the power. I will...

_____

_____

_____

_____

_____

_____

_____

_____

_____

_____

_____

_____

_____

_____

_____

_____

_____

_____

Today in 1938, California Congresswoman Maxine Waters was born in St. Louis, Missouri. She was elected in 1991 and has been an outspoken critic of injustice and racism in government.

I'm curious! What were her jobs before entering politics?

August 16

"My goal was to achieve maximum respect and recognition by my peers, the industry and the public, thereby expanding opportunities for future Black Americans." ~ Georg Olden

Those who came before me did so that I could. I will expand opportunities for others because ...

_____

_____

_____

_____

_____

_____

_____

_____

_____

_____

_____

_____

_____

_____

_____

_____

_____

_____

Today in 1963, graphic designer Georg Olden's Emancipation stamp went on sale to commemorate the hundredth anniversary of the Proclamation. He was the first Black man to design a stamp.

I'm curious! What was the design of the stamp?

August 17

"A people without the knowledge of their past history, origin and culture is like a tree without roots." ~ Marcus Garvey

I am a rooted tree! My roots are important because they...

_____

_____

_____

_____

_____

_____

_____

_____

_____

_____

_____

_____

_____

_____

_____

_____

_____

_____

Today in 1887, activist Marcus Garvey was born in Jamaica. As founder of the UNIA, he believed that Black people needed to secure financial independence from white-dominant society.

I'm curious! What was UNIA an acronym for?

August 18

"Nothing is a bigger waste of time than regretting the past and worrying about the future." ~ James Meredith

I will build upon my past and look forward to my future. I'm looking forward to...

_____

_____

_____

_____

_____

_____

_____

_____

_____

_____

_____

_____

_____

_____

_____

_____

_____

_____

Today in 1963, James Meredith, the first African American admitted to the University of Mississippi, graduated. In 1966, he planned a solo two hundred twenty-mile March Against Fear to highlight continuing racism.

I'm curious! What happened the second day of the March?

August 19

"Wean yourselves from the narrow prejudices and put your souls in their souls stead, thus shall your hearts be enlarged with kindness and benevolence toward them." ~ Benjamin Banneker

I will put myself in the shoes of others so that I may be kind.
To put myself in the shoes of others means to... _____

_____

_____

_____

_____

_____

_____

_____

_____

_____

_____

_____

_____

_____

_____

_____

_____

_____

_____

Today in 1791, surveyor and astrologist Benjamin Banneker sent a letter to President Jefferson along with a copy of his almanac. His letter highlighted slavery's hypocrisy and plead for justice.

I'm curious! Did President Jefferson respond?

August 20
"Suo Marte (By one's own toil, effort, courage)."
~ Wilberforce Universsity's motto

I will work and have courage. Being courageous means...

_____

_____

_____

_____

_____

_____

_____

_____

_____

_____

_____

_____

_____

_____

_____

_____

_____

_____

_____

Today in 1856, Wilberforce University was founded in Central Ohio. It was founded by members of the AME Church and is the first college to be owned and operated by African Americans.

I'm curious! What school was formed from a split with the state?

August 21
"I was chosen by God to lead them from bondage." ~ Nat Turner

I was chosen by God to...

_____

_____

_____

_____

_____

_____

_____

_____

_____

_____

_____

_____

_____

_____

_____

_____

_____

_____

Today in 1831, revolutionary and enslaved preacher Nat Turner led a four-day rebellion of enslaved people in Virginia. He went from plantation to plantation freeing people along the way.

I'm curious! Which item of his is on display at the National Museum of African American History and Culture?

August 22

"Fisk was a site of the birth of a great movement, many great people have emerged from here." ~ Congressman John Lewis

I honor Historically Black Colleges and Universities. HBCUs are important to me and my people because...

_____

_____

_____

_____

_____

_____

_____

_____

_____

_____

_____

_____

_____

_____

_____

_____

_____

_____

Today in 1867, Fisk University was incorporated. Notable alumni include Marion Barry, Johnnetta B. Cole, W. E.B. Du Bois, Nikki Giovanni, Matthew Knowles, John Lewis, and Ida B. Wells.

I'm curious! What national historical landmark is on Fisk's campus?

August 23

"Everything negative—pressure, challenges—is all an opportunity for me to rise." ~ Kobe Bryant

Maya Angelou taught us that no matter what terrible things happen to us we can still rise. I will rise because...

_____

_____

_____

_____

_____

_____

_____

_____

_____

_____

_____

_____

_____

_____

_____

_____

_____

_____

Today in 1978, philanthropist, businessman, and basketball great Kobe Bryant was born in Philadelphia. He played his entire twenty-year career with the Los Angeles Lakers.

I'm curious! For which college did he play basketball?

August 24

"The doors have not been opened, but they have been unlocked. If we press against them, they will open." ~ Edith S. Sampson

I will press against doors until they open and I will...

_____

_____

_____

_____

_____

_____

_____

_____

_____

_____

_____

_____

_____

_____

_____

_____

_____

_____

_____

Today in 1950, Judge Edith S. Sampson was the first Black U.S. delegate appointed to the United Nations. She was also the first Black woman to graduate from Loyola University School of Law and be elected as a judge in Illinois.

I'm curious! Why would she preside over as many as one hundred cases in a day?

August 25
"No matter what accomplishments you make, somebody helped you."
~ Althea Gibson

Somebody has helped me and I will help somebody because...

_____

_____

_____

_____

_____

_____

_____

_____

_____

_____

_____

_____

_____

_____

_____

_____

_____

Today in 1927, tennis great Althea Gibson was born in Clarendon County, South Carolina. In 1957, she became the first African American to win Wimbledon. In all, she won eleven Grand Slam tournaments.

I'm curious! In what other sport did she excel?

August 26

"I don't have a feeling of inferiority. Never had. I'm as good as anybody, but no better." ~ Katherine Johnson

I am my own competition! I'm as good as anybody. Being my own competition means that...

_____

_____

_____

_____

_____

_____

_____

_____

_____

_____

_____

_____

_____

_____

_____

_____

_____

_____

Today in 1918, mathematician Katherine Johnson was born in White Sulpher Spring, Virginia. Her calculations of orbital mechanics at NASA were critical to the success of U.S. spaceflights.

I'm curious! What 2016 movies featured her and her accomplishments?

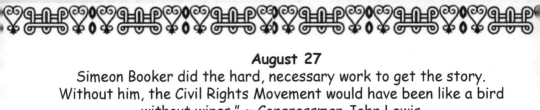

August 27

Simeon Booker did the hard, necessary work to get the story.
Without him, the Civil Rights Movement would have been like a bird
without wings." ~ Congressman John Lewis

I'll do the hard, necessary work to achieve...

_____

_____

_____

_____

_____

_____

_____

_____

_____

_____

_____

_____

_____

_____

_____

_____

_____

_____

_____

Today in 1918, journalist Simeon Booker was born in Baltimore,
Maryland. He was the first Black reporter for the Washington Post
and served as Jet Magazine's Washington bureau chief for forty-
eight years.

I'm curious! What award was he the first Black journalist to win?

August 28

"I say to you today, my friends, that in spite of the difficulties and frustrations of the moment, I still have a dream."
~ Dr. Martin Luther King Jr.

Even when I'm frustrated, I will maintain my dream. I dream about...

_____

_____

_____

_____

_____

_____

_____

_____

_____

_____

_____

_____

_____

_____

_____

_____

_____

_____

Today in 1963, Dr. King delivered his "I Have A Dream" speech at the Lincoln Memorial during the March on Washington. Approximately two hundred fifty thousand people were in attendance.

I'm curious! What other activists were present?

August 29

"If you want to make the world a better place, take a look at yourself, then make that change." ~ Michael Jackson

I want to make the world a better place. To me, a better world is a world where...

_____

_____

_____

_____

_____

_____

_____

_____

_____

_____

_____

_____

_____

_____

_____

_____

_____

_____

Today in 1958, Michael Jackson was born. He is regarded as one of the greatest entertainers in the history of music and one of the most significant cultural figures of the twentieth century.

I'm curious! What song did he co-write to help raise money to end hunger in Africa?

August 30
"Muffle your rage. Get smart instead of muscular." ~ Roy Wilkins

I'm getting smarter every day. I can use my genius to accomplish...

_____

_____

_____

_____

_____

_____

_____

_____

_____

_____

_____

_____

_____

_____

_____

_____

_____

_____

Today in 1901, Roy Wilkins was born in St. Louis, Missouri. He led the NAACP from 1964-1977. He was also a co-founder of the Leadership Conference on Civil Rights and active at the March on Washington.

I'm curious! What honors have been bestowed upon him?

August 31

"You either have to be part of the solution, or you're going to be part of the problem." ~ Eldridge Cleaver

I am part of the solution! I can be helpful by...

_____

_____

_____

_____

_____

_____

_____

_____

_____

_____

_____

_____

_____

_____

_____

_____

_____

_____

_____

Today in 1935, activist Eldridge Cleaver was born in Wabbaseka, Arkansas. He wrote Soul on Ice, was a prominent member of the Black Panthers and served as the editor of their official newspaper.

I'm curious! What political office did he run for in 1968?

September 1

"Armed with your bags of knowledge, understanding, and desire, when they crack that door, step in and take charge."
~ Mother James

I will step in and take charge! When I take charge I will...

_____

_____

_____

_____

_____

_____

_____

_____

_____

_____

_____

_____

_____

_____

_____

_____

_____

_____

_____

Today in 1975, fighter pilot Daniel "Chappie" James Jr. became the first African American to reach the rank of four-star general. He graduated from Tuskegee University and fought in the Korean War.

I'm curious! What are some of the awards and honors that he earned?

September 2
"I want to see how life can triumph." ~ Romare Bearden

I will be triumphant at...

_____

_____

_____

_____

_____

_____

_____

_____

_____

_____

_____

_____

_____

_____

_____

_____

_____

_____

_____

Today in 1911, artist Romare Bearden was born in Charlotte, North Carolina. He was an author, songwriter, and painter but was most famous for his world-renowned, socially conscious collages.

I'm curious! What high honor was he given in 1987?

September 3
"It is easier to build strong children than to repair broken men."
~ Frederick Douglass

I am a builder. I want to build...

_____

_____

_____

_____

_____

_____

_____

_____

_____

_____

_____

_____

_____

_____

_____

_____

_____

_____

_____

Today in 1838, Frederick Douglass escaped from slavery disguised as a sailor. He went on to be a social reformer, writer, speaker, and abolitionist.

I'm curious! What was the name of his autobiography?

September 4

"That was my top priority a proper founders' monument to be erected in the plaza." ~ Miriam Matthews, Historian

I will acknowledge my ancestors. One of my ancestors that I admire is...

_____

_____

_____

_____

_____

_____

_____

_____

_____

_____

_____

_____

_____

_____

_____

_____

_____

_____

Today in 1781, Los Angeles, California was founded by forty-four settlers, of whom at least twenty-six were descendants of Africans. Blacks were free and did not face legal discrimination until after California was acquired by the U.S. in 1848.

I'm curious! How did the Gold Rush impact Blacks in California?

September 5

"Pity and love know little severance. One attends the other."
~ Harriet E. Wilson

I will love and not pity because...

_____

_____

_____

_____

_____

_____

_____

_____

_____

_____

_____

_____

_____

_____

_____

_____

_____

_____

_____

Today in 1859, Our Nig: Sketches From the Life of a Free Black was the first novel published by a Black woman. It is an autobiographical novel by Harriet E. Wilson about her life in New England.

I'm curious! What professor rediscovered the novel in 1981?

September 6

"I would like to be remembered for changing the spirit of the people of this city...." ~ Walter E. Washington

I will be remembered for...

_____

_____

_____

_____

_____

_____

_____

_____

_____

_____

_____

_____

_____

_____

_____

_____

_____

_____

_____

Today in 1967, President Lyndon Johnson named Walter E. Washington commissioner and "unofficial" mayor of Washington, D.C. He then went on to be elected as the first Black mayor of a major city.

I'm curious! From which college did he earn two degrees?

September 7

"We conclude that, in the field of public education, the doctrine of 'separate but equal' has no place." ~ Supreme Court of the U.S.

I am not less than anyone! I am...

_____

_____

_____

_____

_____

_____

_____

_____

_____

_____

_____

_____

_____

_____

_____

_____

_____

_____

Today in 1954, integration of public schools began in Washington, D.C. and Maryland. On May 17, 1954, the Supreme Court judged that racial segregation in public schools was unconstitutional.

I'm curious! What was the name of the U.S. Supreme Court Case?

September 8
"Don't follow the path. Go where there is no path and begin the trail."
~ Ruby Bridges

Just like Ruby, I will begin trails! One trail will be...

_____
_____
_____
_____
_____
_____
_____
_____
_____
_____
_____
_____
_____
_____
_____
_____
_____

Today in 1954, civil rights activist Ruby Bridges was born in Tylertown, Mississippi. She made history when she desegregated a white elementary school in New Orleans, Louisiana.

I'm curious! Who escorted her to school to protect her from racist crowds?

September 9

"I write to keep in contact with our ancestors and to spread truth to people." ~ Sonia Sanchez

Our truths must be told! I will spread truth about...

_____

_____

_____

_____

_____

_____

_____

_____

_____

_____

_____

_____

_____

_____

_____

_____

_____

_____

_____

Today in 1934, poet Sonia Sanchez was born in Birmingham, Alabama. She has authored short stories, essays, plays, and children's books and been an advocate for the rights of oppressed women and minorities.

I'm curious! What are the names of some of her poems?

September 10
"Freedom and free institutions should be as broad as our continent."
~ John Mercer Langston

Freedom is everything, which means...

_____

_____

_____

_____

_____

_____

_____

_____

_____

_____

_____

_____

_____

_____

_____

_____

_____

_____

Today in 1854, John Mercer Langston became the first African
American to pass the bar in Ohio and the first to hold an office when
he was elected town clerk in Brownhelm.

I'm curious! What two major accomplishments followed?

September 11

"His untiring zeal in the cause of education for the colored race...one of the leading spirits of his Presbytery." ~ Frank Leslie

I have untiring zeal to...

_____
_____
_____
_____
_____
_____
_____
_____
_____
_____
_____
_____
_____
_____
_____
_____
_____
_____
_____

Today in 1885, Moses A. Hopkins was appointed minister to Liberia. He was born into slavery in Virginia and later became an educator and established a church and a school in North Carolina.

I'm curious! What school did he become the first Black graduate of?

September 12

"Awards become corroded, friends gather no dust." ~ Jesse Owens

I will always value my friends. Some characteristics of a valuable friend are...

_____

_____

_____

_____

_____

_____

_____

_____

_____

_____

_____

_____

_____

_____

_____

_____

_____

_____

_____

Today in 1913, track star Jesse Owens was born in Oakville, Alabama.
He won eight individual NCAA championships while at Ohio State
University. In 1936, he won four gold medals, becoming the most
successful athlete at the games.

I'm curious! What did he do to make Adolf Hitler angry?

September 13

"The younger generation comes, bringing its gifts. They are the first fruits of the Negro Renaissance." ~ Alain L. Locke

I come, bringing my gifts. My gifts are my talents and they are...

_____

_____

_____

_____

_____

_____

_____

_____

_____

_____

_____

_____

_____

_____

_____

_____

_____

_____

_____

Today in 1885, philosopher Alain LeRoy Locke was born in Philadelphia, Pennsylvania. Often called the Dean of the Harlem Renaissance, he was highly influential to many artists of that time.

I'm curious! What international scholarship did he receive?

September 14

"Lack of encouragement never deterred me. I was the kind of person who would not be put down." ~ Constance Baker Motley

I will not be put down! I will rise and I will...

_____

_____

_____

_____

_____

_____

_____

_____

_____

_____

_____

_____

_____

_____

_____

_____

_____

_____

Today in 1921, activist Constance Baker Motley was born in New Haven, Connecticut. She was an assistant to Thurgood Marshall when he was a New York state senator, and the first Black woman appointed as a federal judge.

I'm curious! With which case did she assist Thurgood Marshall?

September 15

"May men learn to replace bitterness and violence with love and understanding." ~ Sixteenth Street Baptist Bombing Memorial

I will demonstrate love and understanding by...

_____

_____

_____

_____

_____

_____

_____

_____

_____

_____

_____

_____

_____

_____

_____

_____

_____

_____

_____

Today in 1963, four little Black girls were killed when four white supremacists bombed the Sixteenth Street Baptist Church in Birmingham, Alabama. Twenty-two others were injured.

I'm curious! What are the names of three of his television documentaries?

September 16

"There are just so many stories that are buried on family trees."
~ Henry Louis Gates

I will unbury the stories on my family tree and keep them alive because...

_____

_____

_____

_____

_____

_____

_____

_____

_____

_____

_____

_____

_____

_____

_____

_____

_____

_____

Today in 1950, Henry Louis Gates was born in Keyser, West Virginia.
He has written extensively on African American studies, produced
television series on history and genealogy, and lectured around
the world.

I am a symbol of racial uplift! To uplift my race means that I...curious!
What are the names of three of his television documentaries?

September 17

"The greatness of nations is shown by their strict regard for human rights...." ~ Mary Burnett Talbert

I have human rights. My rights are...

_____

_____

_____

_____

_____

_____

_____

_____

_____

_____

_____

_____

_____

_____

_____

_____

_____

_____

Today in 1866, orator and activist, Mary Talbert was born in Oberlin, Ohio. She lectured for women's rights and against racism. She was also the national director of the NAACP anti-lynching campaign.

I'm curious! What did she lecture about in eleven European nations?

September 18

"Cooper and his team became the voice of the urban Black bourgeoisie and a symbol of racial uplift." ~ William Barlow

I am a symbol of racial uplift! To uplift my race means that I...

_____

_____

_____

_____

_____

_____

_____

_____

_____

_____

_____

_____

_____

_____

_____

_____

_____

Today in 1888, Jack L. Cooper was born in Memphis, Tennessee. He was the first African American radio DJ. The All Negro Hour premiered in Chicago in 1929 and was one of the first to play gramophone records on air.

I'm curious! What were some of his other jobs before radio?

September 19

"The development & perpetuation of Scholarship, Leadership, Citizenship, Fidelity, and Brotherhood among Men."
~ Purpose Statement for Iota Phi Theta

I am a scholar and a leader. I will be known for...

_____

_____

_____

_____

_____

_____

_____

_____

_____

_____

_____

_____

_____

_____

_____

_____

_____

_____

Today in 1963, Iota Phi Theta Fraternity, Inc. was founded at Morgan State College (now University) in Baltimore, Maryland. It was founded by twelve men as a support system for militant men of color in the era's turbulent social climate.

I'm curious! What other impactful events happened in 1963?

September 20

"A woman is entitled to have a mood, any mood, a happy mood, a sad mood, an angry mood, whenever she likes" ~ Claire Huxtable

I am entitled to my mood. It is important for me to own my m
ood and my feelings because...

_____

_____

_____

_____

_____

_____

_____

_____

_____

_____

_____

_____

_____

_____

_____

_____

_____

_____

_____

Today in 1984, The Cosby Show premiered on NBC and focused on an upper-middle-class African American family headed by a physician and an attorney along with their five children.

I'm curious! What are some of the awards the show won?

September 21

"He created a considerable uproar upon his arrival and remained the center of attention throughout his stay."
~ Lieutenant Commander R.L. Field

I will create a considerable uproar for what I believe in! I believe in...

_____

_____

_____

_____

_____

_____

_____

_____

_____

_____

_____

_____

_____

_____

_____

_____

_____

_____

_____

Today in 1872, the first Black student was admitted to the Annapolis Naval Academy. At sixteen years old, James H. Conyers was nominated as a candidate by Congressman Robert Elliott.

I'm curious! Why did he resign in October 1873?

September 22

"Discrimination will exist until Americans appreciate the worth and dignity of African Americans." ~ G.W. Murray

I have worth and dignity! This means that I...

_____

_____

_____

_____

_____

_____

_____

_____

_____

_____

_____

_____

_____

_____

_____

_____

_____

Today in 1853, George W. Murray was born into slavery in Sumter County, South Carolina. In 1893, he was elected as a U.S. congressman. After his election, a new state constitution disenfranchised Black citizens.

I'm curious! When did South Carolina elect their next Black congressman?

September 23

"I cannot help wondering what I might have become if I lived in a country which had not handicapped me" ~ Mary Church Terrell

I will not be handicapped because I am determined to...

_____

_____

_____

_____

_____

_____

_____

_____

_____

_____

_____

_____

_____

_____

_____

_____

_____

_____

Today in 1863, Mary Church Terrell was born in Memphis, Tennessee. She was one of the first African American women to earn a college degree, graduating from Oberlin College in 1884.

I'm curious! What organization did she help to found in Washington, D.C.?

September 24

"African American history is central to the American story. How we've wrested triumph from tragedy." ~ President Barack Obama

I am American history and my voice will be heard! About me they will say...

_____

_____

_____

_____

_____

_____

_____

_____

_____

_____

_____

_____

_____

_____

_____

_____

_____

_____

Today in 2016, the National Museum of African American History and Culture opened in Washington, D.C. There are more than forty thousand objects in its collection, and three thousand five hundred items on display.

I'm curious! What is its visitation ranking among the Smithsonians?

September 25

"What we do is more important than what we say or what we say we believe." ~ bell hooks

What I do is most important. I understand that this means...

_____

_____

_____

_____

_____

_____

_____

_____

_____

_____

_____

_____

_____

_____

_____

_____

_____

_____

_____

_____

Today in 1952, author bell hooks, was born in Hopkinsville, Kentucky. Her writing has focused on the intersectionality of race, capitalism, and gender and modern systems of oppression and class domination.

I'm curious! Why does bell hooks write her name using lower case letters?

September 26

"One of the greatest things I fear is letting down my people. I wouldn't live with that type of conscience" ~ Winnie Mandela

I will not let down my people so I will show my greatness by...

_____
_____
_____
_____
_____
_____
_____
_____
_____
_____
_____
_____
_____
_____
_____
_____
_____
_____

Today in 1936, Winnie Mandela was born in South Africa. She was an anti-apartheid activist and member of the Parliament of South Africa. She was married to President Mandela for thirty-eight years.

I'm curious! What was her original profession?

September 27

"Life is like a trumpet, if you don't put anything into it, you don't get anything out." ~ W.C. Handy

I will put everything into my life because...

_____

_____

_____

_____

_____

_____

_____

_____

_____

_____

_____

_____

_____

_____

_____

_____

_____

_____

Today in 1912, Memphis Blues, the first blues composition was published. It was written by W.C. Handy who was considered one of the most influential songwriters in the U.S. The blues became the foundation for many other genres of music.

I'm curious! At which HBCU did he teach?

September 28

"America is more our country, than it is the whites—we have enriched it with our blood and tears." ~ David Walker

This is my country and I will continue to enrich it by...

_____

_____

_____

_____

_____

_____

_____

_____

_____

_____

_____

_____

_____

_____

_____

_____

_____

_____

Today in 1796, abolitionist David Walker was born in Cape Fear, North Carolina. With the assistance of the Prince Hall Masons, he published An Appeal to the Coloured Citizens of the World, a call for unity and slavery's end.

I'm curious! Why did Southern officials punish Appeal distributors?

September 29

"What sweeter triumph could a man wish for himself, his race and his country." ~ Mulzac, on his first captain's voyage

There is a lot for my people to be proud of! I will be proud of my triumphs because...

_____

_____

_____

_____

_____

_____

_____

_____

_____

_____

_____

_____

_____

_____

_____

_____

_____

_____

Today in 1942, Hugh Mulzac, the first Black captain of a U.S. merchant ship launches with the SS Booker T. Washington, the first ship to be named after an African American.

I'm curious! What were his other firsts?

September 30

"He was a natural born talent, born for the stage, but it only lasted for a short time." ~ Richard Barrett

I am a natural born talent! My talents are...

_____
_____
_____
_____
_____
_____
_____
_____
_____
_____
_____
_____
_____
_____
_____
_____
_____
_____

Today in 1942, entertainer Frankie Lymon was born in Harlem, NY. He was the lead singer of the group the Teenagers and had his biggest hit at age thirteen. The group was the model for the Jackson 5.

I'm curious! What was the name of his biggest hit?

October 1

"Hang on to the world as it spins around, just don't let the spin get you down." ~ Donny Hathaway

My ancestors fought and sacrificed so that I could be free. With my freedom I will...

_____

_____

_____

_____

_____

_____

_____

_____

_____

_____

_____

_____

_____

_____

_____

_____

_____

_____

Today in 1945, singer-songwriter and keyboardist Donny Hathaway was born in Chicago, Illinois. He attended Howard University. His musical genius lives on in his daughter, R&B great Lalah Hathaway.

I'm curious! Who gave him a lifetime achievement award?

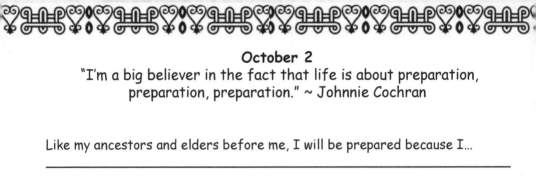

October 2

"I'm a big believer in the fact that life is about preparation, preparation, preparation." ~ Johnnie Cochran

Like my ancestors and elders before me, I will be prepared because I...

_____

_____

_____

_____

_____

_____

_____

_____

_____

_____

_____

_____

_____

_____

_____

_____

_____

_____

_____

Today is 1937, lawyer Johnnie Cochran was born in Shreveport, Louisiana. He was known for his dynamic skills in the courtroom and as an early advocated for police brutality victims.

I'm curious! Who inspired him to practice law?

October 3

"He remained unassuming and unpretentious, in spite of his meteoric success over the years." ~ Donna Halper

I'll remain unpretentious because...

_____

_____

_____

_____

_____

_____

_____

_____

_____

_____

_____

_____

_____

_____

_____

_____

_____

_____

Today in 1949, the first radio station owned and programmed by Black people was established in Atlanta. Jesse B. Blayton Sr., Georgia's first' Black certified account, purchased WERD for $50,000. It was in the same building as the Southern Christian Leadership Conference.

I'm curious! How would MLK signal that he had a radio announcement?

October 4
"Never again will Black women be disregarded." ~ C. Delores Tucker

Black women matter! I can make sure that Black women will not be disregarded by...

_____

_____

_____

_____

_____

_____

_____

_____

_____

_____

_____

_____

_____

_____

_____

_____

_____

Today in 1927, C. Delores Tucker was born in Philadelphia. She became the first Black female secretary of a state in the US and was responsible for the appointment of more women and Blacks than ever before.

I'm curious! Why were so many rappers mad at her?

October 5
"Education remains the key to both economic and political empowerment." ~ Barbara Jordan

Some ways that I can keep empowering myself through education are...

_____

_____

_____

_____

_____

_____

_____

_____

_____

_____

_____

_____

_____

_____

_____

_____

_____

_____

Today in 1995, politician and civil rights leader Barbara Jordan was the first African American and the second woman to accept the Sylvanus Thayer Award for her service and accomplishments.

I'm curious! What must you exemplify to receive this honor?

October 6

"Never to forget where we came from and always praise the bridges that carried us over." ~ Fannie Lou Hamer

I will never forget where I came from because it impacts where I am going. I am going...

_____

_____

_____

_____

_____

_____

_____

_____

_____

_____

_____

_____

_____

_____

_____

_____

_____

_____

Today in 1917, activist and community organizer Fannie Lou Hamer was born in Mississippi. She suffered severe harassment and brutality for her activism and attempts to register herself and others to vote.

I'm curious!   What organizations did she help to found?

October 7

"People must be taught knowledge of self. Then will they be able to understand that which surrounds them" ~ Elijah Muhammad

I know myself. I am …

_____

_____

_____

_____

_____

_____

_____

_____

_____

_____

_____

_____

_____

_____

_____

_____

_____

_____

_____

Today in 1897, Elijah Muhammad was born. He was the leader of the Nation of Islam and mentored Louis Farrakhan, Malcolm X, and Muhammad Ali. His program for economic development led to tremendous growth.

I'm curious! What are the names of some of his written works?

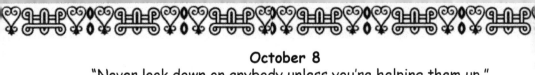

October 8
"Never look down on anybody unless you're helping them up."
~ Rev. Jesse Jackson

To lift as I climb means...

_____

_____

_____

_____

_____

_____

_____

_____

_____

_____

_____

_____

_____

_____

_____

_____

_____

_____

Today in 1941, civil rights activist Rev. Jesse Jackson Sr. was born in South Carolina. He graduated from North Carolina A&T and worked for Dr. King in the SCLC. He also founded Rainbow/PUSH.

I'm curious! What years did he run for president?

October 9
"Tout le sang qui coule rouge: All blood runs red.." ~ Eugene Bullard

All blood runs red, no one is better than me and I am not better than them. To be equal means...

_____

_____

_____

_____

_____

_____

_____

_____

_____

_____

_____

_____

_____

_____

_____

_____

_____

_____

Today in 1895, combat pilot Eugene Bullard was born. He was the first Black military pilot and the only African American to fly in World War II. His honors from the US came after his death.

I'm curious! Why did he stow away on a ship to Europe as a teen?

October 10

"The things that I prize like the stars in the sky are all free. I've got plenty of nothing and nothing is plenty for me"
~ George Gershwin

I value things that cannot be purchased. Things like...

_____

_____

_____

_____

_____

_____

_____

_____

_____

_____

_____

_____

_____

_____

_____

_____

_____

_____

Today in 1935, Gershwin's Porgy and Bess premiered on Broadway in New York City. It featured a cast of classically trained, Black opera singers and was not initially well accepted.

I'm curious! When did it gain new popularity?

October 11

"The creations of African American inventors have changed our world." ~ McKenzie Jean-Philippe

I am a world changer! To be a world changer means...

_____

_____

_____

_____

_____

_____

_____

_____

_____

_____

_____

_____

_____

_____

_____

_____

_____

_____

_____

Today in 1887, Alexander Miles received a patent for automatically opening and closing elevator doors. He got the idea after his daughter fell down an elevator shaft.

I'm curious! How did he earn a living?

October 12

"Once I realized the value of making people laugh, I got very good at it. Fast. ~ Dick Gregory

There is value in what I'm good at. I'm good at ...

_____
_____
_____
_____
_____
_____
_____
_____
_____
_____
_____
_____
_____
_____
_____
_____
_____
_____

Today in 1932, activist Dick Gregory was born. He was a writer, and civil rights activist protesting many injustices including Jim Crow laws, apartheid, and the Vietnam War.

I'm curious! How did he first become well known?

October 13

"If I become a pilot, every Black man can become anything he wants to be in the Navy. I'm the beginning of things to come."
~ Jesse Brown

I'm the beginning of things to come! I'm the beginning of...

_____

_____

_____

_____

_____

_____

_____

_____

_____

_____

_____

_____

_____

_____

_____

_____

_____

_____

Today in 1926, Naval Officer Jesse Leroy Brown was born in Hattiesburg, Mississippi. He was the first African American aviator to complete the Navy's basic flight training program.

I'm curious! How many combat missions did he fly in Korea?

October 14

"Beauty of genuine brotherhood & peace is more precious than diamonds, silver or gold." ~ Martin Luther King Jr.

Peace is precious. To me, peace means...

_____

_____

_____

_____

_____

_____

_____

_____

_____

_____

_____

_____

_____

_____

_____

_____

_____

_____

Today in 1964, Dr. Martin Luther King Jr. was the youngest person to ever receive the Nobel Peace Prize. It was awarded for his nonviolent resistance to racial prejudice in America.

I'm curious! How old was he when he received the award?

October 15

"It seemed like everybody was against us, it was like we were villains."
~ Tony McGee

I am not a villain and I will fight for what is right! I will fight for...

_____

_____

_____

_____

_____

_____

_____

_____

_____

_____

_____

_____

_____

_____

_____

_____

_____

_____

Today in 1969, the Wyoming Black 14 protest began. This led to fourteen members of University of Wyoming's football team being expelled and defunded for requesting to wear black armbands to protest at their game.

I'm curious! What were they protesting?

October 16

"Hug your brother and tell him you love him and let's carry this love all the way back home and never let it die." ~ Louis Farrakhan

I love my brothers and sisters! I show them love by...

_____

_____

_____

_____

_____

_____

_____

_____

_____

_____

_____

_____

_____

_____

_____

_____

_____

_____

Today in 1995, the Million Man March was held in Washington, D.C. The March was called by Minister Louis Farrakhan and directed by Dr. Benjamin Chavis to unite against economic and social ills plaguing the Black community.

I'm curious! Who were some of the prominent speakers at the March?

October 17

"Historians are responsible not only for the words they write but for the words they don't write." ~ Lerone Bennett

I will tell the full story. In order to tell the full story I must...

_____

_____

_____

_____

_____

_____

_____

_____

_____

_____

_____

_____

_____

_____

_____

_____

_____

_____

_____

Today in 1928, scholar Lerone Bennett Jr. was born. He was known for his writings on race relations and his book Before the Mayflower. He was an Essence Magazine editor for over 50 years.

I'm curious! From which college did he graduate?

October 18

"Language and how we use language determines how we act, and how we act then determines our lives and other people's lives."
~ Ntozake Shange

My use of language can have positive or negative impacts on my life. I want to encourage a positive impact so I will...

_____

_____

_____

_____

_____

_____

_____

_____

_____

_____

_____

_____

_____

_____

_____

_____

_____

_____

Today in 1948, playwright and poet Ntozake Shange was born in Trenton, New Jersey. She addressed issues related to race and Black Power and wrote the award winning play turned film For Colored Girls.

I'm curious! In Zulu, what does her name mean?

October 19

"The ultimate expression of generosity is not in giving of what you have, but in giving of who you are." ~ Dr. Johnetta Cole

I will give of myself. The parts of my mind and greatness that I can share include...

_____

_____

_____

_____

_____

_____

_____

_____

_____

_____

_____

_____

_____

_____

_____

_____

_____

_____

Today in 1936 Dr. Johnetta Cole was born in Jacksonville, Florida. She served as the president of Spelman and Bennett College. She has also served as the director of the Smithsonian Museum of African Art.

I'm curious! What distinction did her grandfather have in Florida?

October 20

"If you are fortunate to have opportunity, it is your duty to make
sure others have those opportunities as well."
~ Kamala Harris

I know that I am fortunate. I will open doors for others so that they can...

_____

_____

_____

_____

_____

_____

_____

_____

_____

_____

_____

_____

_____

_____

_____

_____

_____

_____

Today in 1964, Vice President Kamala Harris was born in Oakland,
California. She was the first woman and African American to be elected
as attorney general of California and the state's first Black senator.

I'm curious! From which HBCU did she graduate?

October 21

"Before you can make a dream come true, you must first have one."
~ Ronald McNair

I have a dream! I dream about...

_____

_____

_____

_____

_____

_____

_____

_____

_____

_____

_____

_____

_____

_____

_____

_____

_____

_____

Today in 1950, astronaut and physicist Ronald McNair was born in Lake City, South Carolina. He graduated from North Carolina A&T and was the second African American to fly in space. He died on the Space Shuttle Challenger in 1986.

I'm curious! What book was written about an event from his childhood?

October 22
"I consider myself a political revolutionary humanist."
~ Bobby Seale

I am the best person to define myself! I define myself as...

_____

_____

_____

_____

_____

_____

_____

_____

_____

_____

_____

_____

_____

_____

_____

_____

_____

_____

Today in 1936, activist Bobby Seale was born in Liberty, Texas. He and Huey P. Newton co-founded the Black Panther Party to organize the Black community to resist the racism and classism perpetrated by the system.

I'm curious! What is the name of his 1978 autobiography?

October 23
"Owe no man" ~ Walter "Wiley" Jones

I will pay my debts and use credit wisely. It is important for Black people to be financially literate and independent because...

_____

_____

_____

_____

_____

_____

_____

_____

_____

_____

_____

_____

_____

_____

_____

_____

_____

_____

_____

_____

Today in 1886, Wiley Jones opens the first streetcar line in Pine Bluff, Arkansas. He was one of the wealthiest African Americans in the state owning a saloon, horse stables and a race track.

I'm curious! Who owns his streetcar line today?

October 24

"No nation is so great that the world can afford to let it continue to be deliberately unjust, cruel, and unfair toward its own citizens."
~ NAACP

We matter! Black people matter because...

_____

_____

_____

_____

_____

_____

_____

_____

_____

_____

_____

_____

_____

_____

_____

_____

_____

Today in 1947 the NAACP sent to the United Nations (UN) a document titled "An Appeal to the World." The document asked the UN to address human rights violations the U.S. committed against Blacks.

I'm curious! Who authored the document?

October 25

"The future belongs to those who cannot rest while the evil of injustice thrives in the bosom of America." ~ Coretta Scott King

I cannot rest while evil thrives! With my ancestors' shields up I can continue the fight against evil by...

_____

_____

_____

_____

_____

_____

_____

_____

_____

_____

_____

_____

_____

_____

_____

_____

_____

_____

Today in 1958, the Youth March for Integrated Schools was held in Washington, D.C. It was attended by approximately 10,000 people to demonstrate support for efforts to end segregated schools.

I'm curious! Why couldn't Dr. Martin Luther King attend?

October 26

"Faith and prayer are the vitamins of the soul; man cannot live in health without them." ~ Mahalia Jackson

I will ingest vitamins for my soul. Vitamins for my soul are...

_____

_____

_____

_____

_____

_____

_____

_____

_____

_____

_____

_____

_____

_____

_____

_____

_____

Today in 1911, singer and activist Mahalia Jackson was born in New Orleans, Louisiana. She was known as "The Queen of Gospel" because of her powerful voice and thirty recorded albums.

I'm curious! Where was she the first gospel singer to perform?

October 27

"Benjamin Davis, Jr., a hero in war, a leader in peace, a pioneer for freedom, opportunity, and basic human dignity."
~ President Bill Clinton

I will be a hero, a leader, and a pioneer. It will take hard work to achieve this, but I am preparing by...

_____

_____

_____

_____

_____

_____

_____

_____

_____

_____

_____

_____

_____

_____

_____

_____

_____

Today in 1954, Tuskegee Airman Benjamin O. Davis Jr. became the first Black general in the U.S. Air Force. In 1998 he was advanced to four-star general.

I'm curious! What Army distinction did his father have?

October 28

"A separate and distinct flame: an unwavering source of individual self-enlightenment and a beacon of community strength and support."
~ unknown

I am a distinct flame! I am unique and distinct in so many wonderful ways. Some of those ways are...

_____

_____

_____

_____

_____

_____

_____

_____

_____

_____

_____

_____

_____

_____

_____

_____

_____

Today in 1908, the Louisville Free Public Library, Western Colored Branch opened and became the first public library built for and staffed by African Americans. It was also considered an outreach center.

I'm curious! What were some of the features of the branch?

October 29

"A brilliant man, who was uncompromising in his beliefs about creating a more inclusive democracy." ~ Hoda Zaki

It is okay to be both brilliant and uncompromising in my beliefs because...

_____

_____

_____

_____

_____

_____

_____

_____

_____

_____

_____

_____

_____

_____

_____

_____

_____

_____

Today in 1949, Alonzo Moron became the first Black president of Hampton Institute. He graduated from Hampton in 1927 and went on to earn degrees from Brown University and Harvard Law School.

I'm curious! What degree did he earn from Hampton?

October 30

"Black innovators changed the way we live through contributions, from the traffic light to the ironing board." ~ Thad Morgan

I am an innovator. Some of my innovative contributions to my community will be...

_____

_____

_____

_____

_____

_____

_____

_____

_____

_____

_____

_____

_____

_____

_____

_____

_____

_____

_____

Today in 1922, nurse Marie Van Brittan Brown was born in Queens, New York. She invented the home security system and received a patent in 1969 and an award from the National Science Committee.

I'm curious! How did her system work?

October 31

"When you leave, do all you can possibly do to leave it a better place for the folks who come behind you." ~ Earl Lloyd

I am a path maker. Something I want to leave better than how I found it is...

_____

_____

_____

_____

_____

_____

_____

_____

_____

_____

_____

_____

_____

_____

_____

_____

_____

_____

Today in 1950, Earl Lloyd became the first African American to play in an NBA game. He played over five hundred and sixty games for three NBA teams and coached the Detroit Pistons. He was raised in Alexandria, Virginia.

I'm curious! From which HBCU did he graduate?

November 1

"When I see a barrier, I cry and I fuss, and then I get a ladder and climb over it." ~ John H. Johnson

My purpose cannot be stopped! I will remind myself to climb over barriers by...

_____

_____

_____

_____

_____

_____

_____

_____

_____

_____

_____

_____

_____

_____

_____

_____

_____

_____

Today in 1945, the first issue of Ebony magazine was published by John H. Johnson in Chicago, Illinois. The purpose of the magazine was to celebrate African American life and culture.

I'm curious! What else did Johnson Publishing produce?

November 2

"Let us put our money together; let us use our money, and reap the benefit ourselves." ~ Maggie L. Walker

I will work with other Black geniuses. It is important that we work together because...

_____

_____

_____

_____

_____

_____

_____

_____

_____

_____

_____

_____

_____

_____

_____

_____

_____

_____

_____

Today in 1903, Maggie L. Walker founded the St. Luke Penny Savings Bank in Richmond, VA. She was the first Black woman to establish and serve as the president of a bank.

I'm curious! What was the bank called from 1930-2007?

November 3
"Magic lies in challenging what seems impossible."
~ Carol Moseley Braun

I challenge what seems impossible because...

_____
_____
_____
_____
_____
_____
_____
_____
_____
_____
_____
_____
_____
_____
_____
_____
_____
_____
_____

Today in 1992, Carol Moseley Braun became the first female African American senator and first African American senator from the Democratic Party.

I'm curious! What other political offices did she run for?

November 4

"We are the ones we've been waiting for. We are the change that we seek." ~ President Barack Obama

My community is waiting for me because of who I am. They are waiting for me to...

_____

_____

_____

_____

_____

_____

_____

_____

_____

_____

_____

_____

_____

_____

_____

_____

_____

_____

_____

Today in 2008, Barack Obama became the first African American elected as U.S. president. He graduated from Columbia University in 1983 and worked as a community organizer in Chicago, Illinois.

I'm curious! What distinction did he earn while at Harvard?

November 5

"I want history to remember me...not as the first Black woman to have made a bid for the presidency of the United States, but as a Black woman who lived in the twentieth century and who dared to be herself. I want to be remembered as a catalyst for change in America."
~ Shirley Chisholm

I want to be remembered as ...

_____

_____

_____

_____

_____

_____

_____

_____

_____

_____

_____

_____

_____

_____

_____

_____

_____

_____

Today in 1968, Shirley Chisholm become the first Black woman to be elected to Congress. In 1972, she became the first Black candidate for president. In 2015, she was awarded the Presidential Medal of Freedom.

I'm curious! What was her career before politics?

November 6

"Spitefulness and hatred only erode that which is truly magnificent about this country."~ Sharon Pratt Kelly

Spitefulness and hatred have no place in my heart. Instead, my heart is home to...

_____

_____

_____

_____

_____

_____

_____

_____

_____

_____

_____

_____

_____

_____

_____

_____

_____

_____

Today in 1990, Sharon Pratt Kelly was elected mayor of Washington, D.C. She was the first African American woman to serve as mayor of a major American city.

I'm curious! From which HBCU did she earn her BA and JD?

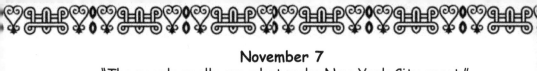

November 7
"The people really are what make New York City great."
~ David Dinkins

I help make my city great by...

_____
_____
_____
_____
_____
_____
_____
_____
_____
_____
_____
_____
_____
_____
_____
_____
_____
_____
_____

Today in 1989, David Dinkins was elected first Black mayor of New
York City. During his tenure, crime was reduced dramatically.
Before becoming mayor, he was recognized as a Montford
Point Marine and is a Howard University Alumnus.

I'm curious! What are three of the boards on which he served?

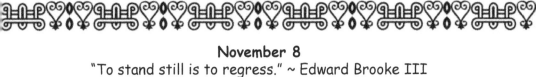

November 8
"To stand still is to regress." ~ Edward Brooke III

I will not stand still! I will be a catalyst for...

_____

_____

_____

_____

_____

_____

_____

_____

_____

_____

_____

_____

_____

_____

_____

_____

_____

_____

Today in 1966, Edward Brooke III became the first African American elected to the U.S. Senate since the period of Reconstruction. He was born in Washington, D.C and earned his BA from Howard University.

I'm curious! What was his other first as an African American?

November 9

"Avoid popularity. It has many snares and no real benefit."
~ Dorothy Dandridge

I would rather do the right thing, than be popular because ...

_____

_____

_____

_____

_____

_____

_____

_____

_____

_____

_____

_____

_____

_____

_____

_____

_____

_____

Today in 1922, Dorothy Dandridge was born in Cleveland, Ohio. She was the first Black actress to be nominated for a Golden Globe and the first to be nominated for an Academy Award for Best Actress.

I'm curious! What are two of her most well-known movies?

November 10

"His appointment jarred the old pros who had become accustomed to Negroes serving only as porters, messengers, and maids"
~ Simeon Booker

I will surprise those who underestimate me. They will realize that I am...

_____

_____

_____

_____

_____

_____

_____

_____

_____

_____

_____

_____

_____

_____

_____

_____

_____

Today in 1960, Andrew T. Hatcher was named associate press secretary by President John F. Kennedy. He was the first African American to hold this position.

I'm curious! What organization did he co-found in 1963?

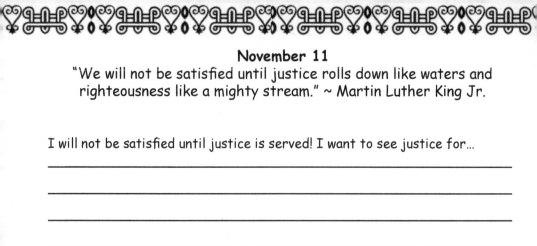

November 11

"We will not be satisfied until justice rolls down like waters and righteousness like a mighty stream." ~ Martin Luther King Jr.

I will not be satisfied until justice is served! I want to see justice for...

_____

_____

_____

_____

_____

_____

_____

_____

_____

_____

_____

_____

_____

_____

_____

_____

_____

_____

Today in 1989, the Civil Rights Memorial was dedicated. It honors forty-one people who were killed from 1954 to 1968 in the struggle for the equal and integrated treatment of all. It represents the aspirations to end segregation.

I'm curious! Where is the memorial located?

November 12

"We visualize a world in which all women and their families reach their full potential in all aspects of life ...."
~ Sigma Gamma Rho Vision Statement

I will reach my full potential! To be sure that I am ready I am...

_____

_____

_____

_____

_____

_____

_____

_____

_____

_____

_____

_____

_____

_____

_____

_____

_____

_____

_____

Today in 1922, Sigma Gamma Rho Sorority, Inc. was founded at Butler University in Indianapolis, Indiana. Their goal is to achieve greater progress in education, health awareness, and leadership.

I'm curious! Who are some of their prominent members?

November 13
"I am where I am because I believe in all possibilities."
~Whoopi Goldberg

I believe in my community. I believe in the power of my ancestors.

_____

_____

_____

_____

_____

_____

_____

_____

_____

_____

_____

_____

_____

_____

_____

_____

_____

_____

Today in 1955, Whoopi Goldberg was born in New York City. She has
acted in over one hundred and fifty films, authored books, hosted
a talk show, and performed in theater. She is the first African
American to win EGOT.

I'm curious! What is EGOT and who else has won this?

November 14

"Each generation has an obligation to pick up the baton. We want young people to take that baton and run with it."
~ Valerie Jarrett

I will pick up the baton and I will run with it! It's important that my generation do this because...

_____

_____

_____

_____

_____

_____

_____

_____

_____

_____

_____

_____

_____

_____

_____

_____

_____

Today in 1956, Valerie Jarrett was born. She worked for Chicago Mayors Harold Washington and John Daley before becoming senior advisor to President Obama and Director of the Office of Public Engagement and Intergovernmental Affairs.

I'm curious! Where was she born?

November 15

"Institute hospitals and training schools. Let us no longer sit idly and inanely deploring existing conditions."
~ Dr. Daniel H. Williams

We can't sit idly, we must be active! I want to be active about...

_____

_____

_____

_____

_____

_____

_____

_____

_____

_____

_____

_____

_____

_____

_____

_____

_____

Today in 1894, Dr. Daniel H. Williams founded Freedmen's Hospital School of Nursing in Washington, D.C. It was the first in the country in a university setting and awarded over 1,587 diplomas until it closed in the 1970s.

I'm curious! What university was the school connected to?

November 16

"Dr. Richard Greener was a leading intellectual
of the time."
~ Henry Louis Gates Jr.

I am intellectual! To me, being intellectual means...

_____

_____

_____

_____

_____

_____

_____

_____

_____

_____

_____

_____

_____

_____

_____

_____

_____

_____

Today in 1873, Richard T. Greener, Harvard's first Black graduate,
was named as the first Black faculty member at the
University of South Carolina.

I'm curious! What school of law did he later serve as dean?

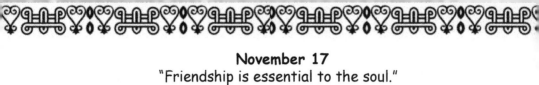

November 17
"Friendship is essential to the soul."
~ Omega Psi Phi Fraternity, Inc. motto

Healthy friendships and support systems are essential to staying positive and productive. Characteristics of healthy friendships are...

_____

_____

_____

_____

_____

_____

_____

_____

_____

_____

_____

_____

_____

_____

_____

_____

_____

_____

Today in 1911, Omega Psi Phi Fraternity, Inc. was founded by three Howard University juniors and their faculty advisor. They were the first fraternity to be founded at an HBCU.

I'm curious! What are their Cardinal Principles?

November 18

"Do not be silent; there is no limit to the power that may be released through you." ~ Dr. Howard Thurman

There is no limit to the power inside of me! I know that there is no limit because...

_____

_____

_____

_____

_____

_____

_____

_____

_____

_____

_____

_____

_____

_____

_____

_____

_____

Today in 1900, Dr. Howard Thurman is born in Daytona Beach, Florida. He was an author, theologian, educator, and civil rights leader serving as a mentor to many, including Martin Luther King Jr. He was also a Morehouse graduate.

I'm curious! What two chapels did he serve as dean?

November 19
"Truth is powerful and it prevails." ~ Sojourner Truth

I will focus on truth. The truth is...

_____

_____

_____

_____

_____

_____

_____

_____

_____

_____

_____

_____

_____

_____

_____

_____

_____

_____

_____

Today in 1797, activist Sojourner Truth was born into slavery in Rifton, New York. She was able to escape with her infant daughter in 1826 and became the first Black woman to win a case to recover her son.

I'm curious! Where is she the first Black woman to have a statue?

November 20

"Whereas such policies result in segregated patterns of housing and
necessarily produce other forms of discrimination"
~ John F. Kennedy

I am equal and I deserve equality. I will fight discrimination by...

_____

_____

_____

_____

_____

_____

_____

_____

_____

_____

_____

_____

_____

_____

_____

_____

_____

_____

_____

Today in 1962, President Kennedy issued an executive order
banning racial discrimination in the sale, leasing,
or rental of federally financed housing.

I'm curious! The passage of what act enforced this order in 1968?

November 21

"For Christ and Humanity—that religion and learning may go hand in hand, and character grow with knowledge."
~ Shaw University motto

My character will grow with my knowledge! To me, this means that...

_____

_____

_____

_____

_____

_____

_____

_____

_____

_____

_____

_____

_____

_____

_____

_____

_____

_____

Today in 1865, Shaw University was established making it the second HBCU in the southern states. The founding presidents of four North Carolina HBCUs were all Shaw University alumni.

I'm curious! What HBCU was located on Shaw's campus for a year?

November 22

"Our mission is to provide timely and compelling news that is informative and relevant to the African American experience."
~ Philadelphia Tribune

I will be timely, compelling, informative, and relevant. In preparation to be all these things I must...

_____

_____

_____

_____

_____

_____

_____

_____

_____

_____

_____

_____

_____

_____

_____

_____

Today in 1884, Christopher Perry published the first copy of the Philadelphia Tribune, the oldest continuously published Black newspaper. The paper is committed to our social, political, and economic advancement.

I'm curious! When he began the paper, what five jobs did he do?

November 23

"John Lee Love is remembered for devising small things to make life easier." ~ Mary Bellis

It's the small things that matter. Some small things that matter to me are...

_____
_____
_____
_____
_____
_____
_____
_____
_____
_____
_____
_____
_____
_____
_____
_____
_____
_____

Today in 1897, John Lee Love received a patent for the portable pencil sharpener. He also invented several additional devices. His design has been in continuous use since it was first produced.

I'm curious! What was his trade?

November 24

"A man whose musical genius served as his weapon in the struggle toward a whole America." ~ John Hope Franklin

I will use my genius to serve others. My genius is my ability to...

_____

_____

_____

_____

_____

_____

_____

_____

_____

_____

_____

_____

_____

_____

_____

_____

_____

_____

Today in 1868, pianist Scott Joplin was born in Texarkana, Texas. He is known as the "King of Ragtime" and wrote over one hundred original pieces, a ballet, and two operas. In 1976, he was awarded a Pulitzer Prize.

I'm curious! What was the name of the Motown movie about his life?

November 25

"Buses are a-comin', oh yes. They're rolling into Jackson, oh yes.
Better get you ready, oh yes." ~ Freedom Song

I'll be ready! I'm ready for...

_____

_____

_____

_____

_____

_____

_____

_____

_____

_____

_____

_____

_____

_____

_____

_____

_____

_____

Today in 1955, the Interstate Commerce Commission banned
segregation in buses and waiting rooms involved in interstate travel.
Some states still segregated state travel and the ban was not fully
enforced until 1961.

I'm curious! What movement helped this ban's enforcement?

November 26

"I pray they will carry on in spite of that dreadful monster prejudice, and with patience, courage, fortitude and perseverance achieve success for themselves" ~ Major Taylor

I will carry on! I must carry on because...

_____

_____

_____

_____

_____

_____

_____

_____

_____

_____

_____

_____

_____

_____

_____

_____

_____

_____

Today in 1878, Marshall "Major" Taylor was born. In 1899, he became the first African American to become cycling world champion and the second to win a world championship in any sport.

I'm curious! How many days was his longest event?

November 27

"When the power of love overcomes the love of power the
world will know peace." ~ Jimi Hendrix

I know the power of love. The power is...

_____

_____

_____

_____

_____

_____

_____

_____

_____

_____

_____

_____

_____

_____

_____

_____

_____

_____

_____

Today in 1942, Jimi Hendrix was born. He was a guitarist, singer,
and songwriter. The Rock and Roll Hall of Fame described him as "the
greatest instrumentalist in the history of rock music."

I'm curious! Who are some of the artists that he played backup for?

November 28

"I have this ability to find hidden talent in people that sometimes even they didn't know they had." ~ Berry Gordy

I find the best in people because...

_____

_____

_____

_____

_____

_____

_____

_____

_____

_____

_____

_____

_____

_____

_____

_____

_____

_____

Today in 1929, record executive Berry Gordy was born in Detroit, Michigan. He founded Motown Records in 1959 and was responsible for racially integrating popular music and many venues.

I'm curious! What are some of the hit songs that he composed?

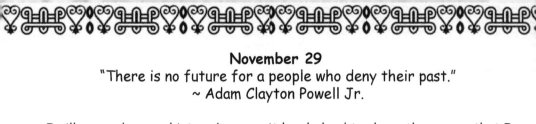

November 29
"There is no future for a people who deny their past."
~ Adam Clayton Powell Jr.

I will never deny my history because it has helped to shape the person that I am. A few things that I love about my history include ...

_____

_____

_____

_____

_____

_____

_____

_____

_____

_____

_____

_____

_____

_____

_____

_____

_____

_____

Today in 1908, Adam Clayton Powell Jr. was born. He was the first African American to be elected to the New York City Council and the first African American from New York elected to Congress.

I'm curious! What church did he pastor from 1937-1971?

November 30

"Enthusiasm is the electricity of life. How do you get it? You act
enthusiastic until you make it a habit." ~ Gordon Parks

I will act enthusiastically about the things that fuel me. I am enthusiastic
about...

_____

_____

_____

_____

_____

_____

_____

_____

_____

_____

_____

_____

_____

_____

_____

_____

_____

_____

_____

Today in 1912, filmmaker Gordon Parks was born. He was a
photojournalist who focused on civil rights, poverty, and glamour. He
was the first African American to produce and direct major films.

I'm curious! Which film genre is he credited with creating?

December 1

"I have learned over the years that when one's mind is made up, this diminishes fear; knowing what must be done does away with fear."
~ Rosa Parks

I will not be afraid! I know that I must...

_____

_____

_____

_____

_____

_____

_____

_____

_____

_____

_____

_____

_____

_____

_____

_____

_____

_____

_____

Today in 1955, Rosa Parks was arrested for refusing to give up her seat on a bus in Montgomery, Alabama. This sparked a bus boycott by African Americans that continued until December 1956.

I'm curious! What happened to end the boycott?

December 2

"I have had a great determination and will never despair because of disappointments." ~ Granville T. Woods

I am determined and will not despair. From my disappointments I have learned...

_____

_____

_____

_____

_____

_____

_____

_____

_____

_____

_____

_____

_____

_____

_____

_____

_____

_____

Today in 1884, Granville T. Woods was granted a patent for a telephone transmitter. Self-taught, he was the first African American to become a mechanical and electrical engineer.

I'm curious! How many patents did he hold?

December 3

"Right is of no sex—Truth is of no color—God is the Father of us all, and we are brethren." ~ North Star motto

Family, both blood and chosen are important. I love my family because...

_____

_____

_____

_____

_____

_____

_____

_____

_____

_____

_____

_____

_____

_____

_____

_____

_____

_____

Today in 1847, Frederick Douglass published the first North Star, an anti-slavery newspaper. The newspaper was four-pages long and sold by subscription at the cost of $2 per year to more than four thousand readers.

I'm curious! How did he earn funds to publish his newspaper?

December 4

"First of all, servants of all, we shall transcend all."
~ Alpha Phi Alpha motto

I will serve my community. One way that I can give back to my community is by...

_____

_____

_____

_____

_____

_____

_____

_____

_____

_____

_____

_____

_____

_____

_____

_____

_____

_____

Today in 1906, Alpha Phi Alpha, the first Black Greek letter fraternity was formed at Cornell University. Their mission is to develop leaders and promote brotherhood and academic excellence.

I'm curious! Who are five prominent Alphas?

December 5
"I'm promised for this world just so long" ~ Bill Pickett

I will make the most out of my time here. Making the most of time here means that I will...

_____

_____

_____

_____

_____

_____

_____

_____

_____

_____

_____

_____

_____

_____

_____

_____

_____

_____

_____

Today in 1870, cowboy Bill Pickett was born in Williamson, Texas. He performed in rodeos and Wild West shows and was known for his tricks and stunts when he traveled around Texas, Arizona, Wyoming, and Oklahoma.

I'm curious! How was he honored in 1993?

December 6

"The will to win, the desire to succeed, the urge to reach your full potential...these are the keys that will unlock the door to personal excellence." ~ Coach Eddie Robinson

I am committed to personal excellence! I will know that I have reached my full potential when...

_____

_____

_____

_____

_____

_____

_____

_____

_____

_____

_____

_____

_____

_____

_____

_____

_____

_____

Today in 1997, Coach Eddie Robinson retired from Grambling University after fifty-six years. His record was 408-165-15. He is one of the greatest and most successful coaches in history with the third most wins.

I'm curious: Why didn't Robinson coach in 1943 and 1944?

December 7

"He [Doris Miller] died for his country so that his people might rise another notch in dignity and courage." ~ Pittsburgh Courier

I rise in dignity and courage. Having dignity and courage means that...

_____

_____

_____

_____

_____

_____

_____

_____

_____

_____

_____

_____

_____

_____

_____

_____

_____

_____

Today in 1941, U.S. Navy Sailor Doris Miller downed three Japanese planes in the attack on Pearl Harbor, with no training. He was the first African American to be awarded the Cross, the third highest Navy honor.

I'm curious: What was Miller's job in the Navy?

December 8

"Savor the moments that are warm and special and giggly."
~ Sammy Davis Jr.

A moment I want to savor was when...

_____

_____

_____

_____

_____

_____

_____

_____

_____

_____

_____

_____

_____

_____

_____

_____

_____

_____

Today in 1925, entertainer Sammy Davis Jr. was born in Harlem, New York. He was a singer, actor, and comedian known for his many impressions and Las Vegas shows. He began performing at three years old.

I'm curious! Which of Davis' body parts was artificial?

December 9
"We were knocked down but not knocked out."
~ Colonel Charles Young

I will not be knocked out! The difference between being knocked down and knocked out is...

_____

_____

_____

_____

_____

_____

_____

_____

_____

_____

_____

_____

_____

_____

_____

_____

_____

_____

Today in 1903, Colonel Charles Young spoke at Stanford University, speaking on issues present at that time, which was a rarity for military officers. He was the first Black national park superintendent, military attaché, and colonel.

I'm curious! What did he do to prove his physical fitness for reinstatement?

December 10

"To make our way, we must have firm resolve, persistence, tenacity.
We must gear ourselves to work hard all the way. We can never let up.
~ Ralph J. Bunche

I have firm resolve, persistence, and tenacity. My actions show that I have all three because...

_____

_____

_____

_____

_____

_____

_____

_____

_____

_____

_____

_____

_____

_____

_____

_____

_____

Today in 1950, Ralph J. Bunche became the first African American awarded the Nobel Peace Prize and the first to earn a PhD in political science. He was also involved in the formation of the United Nations.

I'm curious! What did Dr. Bunche do to earn a Nobel Peace Prize?

December 11

"Morrie Turner changed the face of comics forever when he created Wee Pals." ~ unknown

I will make sure that my people are represented by...

_____

_____

_____

_____

_____

_____

_____

_____

_____

_____

_____

_____

_____

_____

_____

_____

_____

_____

Today in 1923, cartoonist Morrie Turner was born in Oakland, California. He created the Wee Pals, the first American syndicated comic strip with diverse characters, published in 1965.

I'm curious! How many newspapers carried Wee Pals at its peak?

December 12

"Dr. Grant was one of the few Negroes whose brilliancy of achievement in the medical line was recognized by all races."
~ Oswego Palladium

My brilliancy of achievement will be recognized by all! I will be recognized for...

_____

_____

_____

_____

_____

_____

_____

_____

_____

_____

_____

_____

_____

_____

_____

_____

_____

_____

Today in 1899, George F. Grant received a patent for the wooden golf tee. He was also Harvard's first African American professor after graduating from the School of Dental Medicine in 1870.

I'm curious! What association was Grant elected president of?

December 13

"We who believe in freedom cannot rest until it comes." ~ Ella Baker

I believe in freedom for myself and my people. Freedom for us looks like...

_____
_____
_____
_____
_____
_____
_____
_____
_____
_____
_____
_____
_____
_____
_____
_____
_____
_____
_____

Today in 1903, Ella Baker was born. For over fifty years she worked behind the scenes organizing for SNCC, SCLC, & the NAACP becoming one of the most influential women in the movement.

I'm curious! From what college did Ella Baker graduate?

December 14

"When people conclude that all is futile, then the absurd becomes the norm." ~ Stanley Crouch

I will never make the absurd the norm! When something is absurd that means that it is...

_____

_____

_____

_____

_____

_____

_____

_____

_____

_____

_____

_____

_____

_____

_____

_____

_____

_____

_____

Today in 1945, Stanley Crouch was born. As a poet, columnist, and novelist, his works were often controversial, challenging forms of rap and jazz music as well as prominent African Americans.

I'm curious! What are the names of two of Crouch's books?

December 15

"We will have moral stability and justice in society when those who are not the immediate victims of injustice feel as intensely the injustices as the victim himself." ~ Dr. Kenneth Clark

Often times, Black people live in chronic discomfort while white people are comfortable. If they lived a day in our shoes they would learn that...

_____

_____

_____

_____

_____

_____

_____

_____

_____

_____

_____

_____

_____

_____

_____

_____

Today in 1961, Dr. Kenneth Clark was awarded the Spingarn Medal for his research with his wife, Mamie, that influenced the U.S. Supreme Court decision on school desegregation.

I'm curious! What were their studies focused on?

December 16
"We preferred a separate organization of our own...
established after our own ideas and notions." ~ Isaac Lane

Organizations that are established with me in mind are important because...

_____
_____
_____
_____
_____
_____
_____
_____
_____
_____
_____
_____
_____
_____
_____
_____
_____
_____
_____

Today in 1870, the Colored Methodist Episcopal Church was organized in Jackson, Tennessee by forty-one formerly enslaved men and women. In the 1950s, their name was changed from Colored to the Christian.

I'm curious! What church were the founders originally members of?

December 17

"Anything that has to do with money, I want to be in that business." ~ Robert Johnson

Black wealth and philanthropy are important to our independence because...

_____

_____

_____

_____

_____

_____

_____

_____

_____

_____

_____

_____

_____

_____

_____

_____

_____

_____

_____

Today in 2002, Robert Johnson, the first Black billionaire, became the first major sports team owner with his purchase of the Charlotte expansion basketball team, the Bobcats.

I'm curious! Who did he sell the team to in 2010?

December 18

"I find, in being Black, a thing of beauty:
a joy; a strength; a secret cup of gladness." ~ Ossie Davis

Black is beautiful! What makes my Black beautiful is...

_____

_____

_____

_____

_____

_____

_____

_____

_____

_____

_____

_____

_____

_____

_____

_____

_____

_____

Today in 1917, Ossie Davis was born in Cogdell, Georgia. He was an
actor, director, author and civil rights activist who won numerous
awards including the National Medal of Arts.

I'm curious! Who was his wife for fifty-six years?

December 19

"Challenges make you discover things about yourself that you never really knew." ~ Cicely Tyson

I welcome challenges. Through challenges I have learned that...

_____

_____

_____

_____

_____

_____

_____

_____

_____

_____

_____

_____

_____

_____

_____

_____

_____

_____

Today in 1924, actress Cicely Tyson was born in Harlem, New York. She has won awards for her work on television, film, and Broadway. She has won a Tony, Emmys, and the Presidential Medal of Freedom.

I'm curious! What movie did she win two Emmys for in 1974?

December 20

"I'm somebody, and nobody's gonna hold me down...I'm somebody!"
~ Deena Jones in Dreamgirls

I'm somebody and I can't be held down. I will rise up, and I will...

_____

_____

_____

_____

_____

_____

_____

_____

_____

_____

_____

_____

_____

_____

_____

_____

_____

_____

_____

Today in 1981, the musical Dreamgirls premiered on Broadway. It was nominated for thirteen Tony Awards and won six. In 2006 it was adapted into a movie with a star-studded cast.

I'm curious! What is Dreamgirls about?

December 21
"To be called 'African- Americans' has cultural integrity, it puts us in our proper historical context." ~ Rev. Jesse Jackson

I have pride in my culture! Some of the things in my culture that I am proud of include...

_____

_____

_____

_____

_____

_____

_____

_____

_____

_____

_____

_____

_____

_____

_____

_____

_____

_____

Today in 1988, Jesse Jackson, joined by others, called for Americans of African descent to abandon identifiers "colored" and "Black" and to refer to themselves as African American.

I'm curious! Who joined him in announcing this change?

December 22

"There were a lot of closed doors at that time and he was determined to open them in a way that would make people feel good about what they were doing" ~ Gov. Dan Evans

I will open doors and I will feel good doing so because...

_____

_____

_____

_____

_____

_____

_____

_____

_____

_____

_____

_____

_____

_____

_____

_____

_____

_____

Today in 1924, Arthur Fletcher was born. He is referred to as the "father of affirmative action" and was appointed chair of the Commission on Civil Rights where he initiated and supported policies for the hiring of minorities.

I'm curious! For what team was he the first African American to play?

December 23

"Your first duty is to humanity. I want others to look at us and see
that we care not just about ourselves but about others."
~ Madam C.J. Walker

I care about myself and others. To be a humanitarian means to...

_____

_____

_____

_____

_____

_____

_____

_____

_____

_____

_____

_____

_____

_____

_____

_____

_____

_____

Today in 1867, Madam Walker was born. She became the first female
millionaire by developing a line of hair care products for Black women.
She was also an activist and a philanthropist.

I'm curious! Where is her mansion and what has it been used for?

December 24
"for the relief and protection of aged and afflicted Africans."
~ Georgia Infirmary Mission

We stand on the shoulders of our ancestors and our elders. I will take care of my elders by...

_____

_____

_____

_____

_____

_____

_____

_____

_____

_____

_____

_____

_____

_____

_____

_____

_____

Today in 1832, the Georgia Infirmary was chartered. This was the first hospital for African Americans and the first training center for African American nurses.

I'm curious! What is the name and primary use of the Infirmary now?

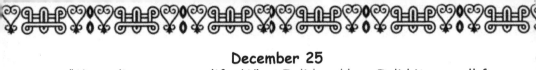

December 25

"My audience was my life. What I did and how I did it, was all for my audience." ~ Cab Calloway

I know my inspiration. I am inspired by...

_____

_____

_____

_____

_____

_____

_____

_____

_____

_____

_____

_____

_____

_____

_____

_____

_____

_____

_____

Today in 1907, Cab Calloway was born in Rochester, New York and had a career that spanned over sixty-five years. He was the first African American to sell a million records and to have a nationally syndicated radio show.

I'm curious! What was the name of his most famous song?

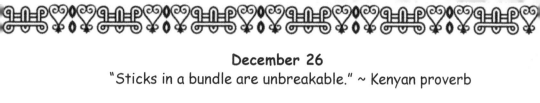

December 26
"Sticks in a bundle are unbreakable." ~ Kenyan proverb

I strive for unity! Together we can...

_____
_____
_____
_____
_____
_____
_____
_____
_____
_____
_____
_____
_____
_____
_____
_____
_____
_____
_____

Today is the first day of Kwanzaa, Umoja (Unity)—To strive for and maintain unity in the family, community, nation, and race.

I'm curious! Who in your family is a unifier?

December 27

"If I didn't define myself for myself, I would be crunched into other people's fantasies for me and eaten alive."
~ Audre Lorde

I define who I am because I am in control of my destiny! I am destined for...

_____

_____

_____

_____

_____

_____

_____

_____

_____

_____

_____

_____

_____

_____

_____

_____

_____

_____

Today is the second day of Kwanzaa, Kujichagulia (Self Determination)—To define ourselves, name ourselves, create for ourselves and speak for ourselves.

I'm curious! Who do you know who has adopted an African name?

December 28

"I know I got it made while the masses of Black people don't, but as long as they ain't free, I ain't free."
~ Muhammad Ali

I will work with others until we all have success! To me, success for my entire community can be described as...

_____

_____

_____

_____

_____

_____

_____

_____

_____

_____

_____

_____

_____

_____

_____

_____

_____

_____

Today is the third day of Kwanzaa, Ujima (Collective Work & Responsibility)—To build and maintain our community together and to make our brother's and sister's problems our own and to solve them together.

I'm curious! What agency is doing good things in your neighborhood?

December 29

"We need to control the economy in our community so that we won't have to boycott other people to get jobs" ~ Malcolm X

I will create and support Black wealth by...

_____
_____
_____
_____
_____
_____
_____
_____
_____
_____
_____
_____
_____
_____
_____
_____
_____
_____
_____

Today is the fourth day of Kwanzaa, Ujamaa (Cooperative Economics)—To build and maintain our own stores, shops and other businesses and to profit from them together.

I'm curious! What is the closest Black owned business to your home?

December 30

"Action, self-reliance, and vision of the future are the only means by which the oppressed have seen and realized freedom."
~ Marcus Garvey

I have a vision for our future! That vision looks like...

_____

_____

_____

_____

_____

_____

_____

_____

_____

_____

_____

_____

_____

_____

_____

_____

_____

_____

_____

Today is the fifth day of Kwanzaa, Nia (Purpose)—To make as our collective vocation the developing of our community in order to restore our people to their traditional greatness.

I'm curious! What organization do you know that is purposeful?

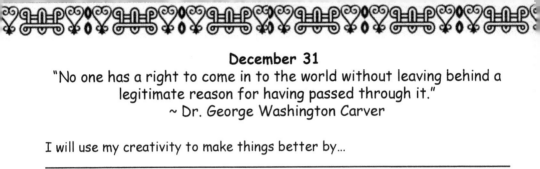

December 31

"No one has a right to come in to the world without leaving behind a legitimate reason for having passed through it."
~ Dr. George Washington Carver

I will use my creativity to make things better by…

_____

_____

_____

_____

_____

_____

_____

_____

_____

_____

_____

_____

_____

_____

_____

_____

_____

_____

_____

Today is the sixth day of Kwanzaa, Kuumba (Creativity)—To always do as much as we can, in the way that we can, in order to leave our community more beautiful than when we inherited it.

I'm curious! Who do you know that embodies Kuumba?

CPSIA information can be obtained
at www.ICGtesting.com
Printed in the USA
JSHW040845011121
20049JS00001B/1

9 780578 806372